THE HAND BUT NOT THE HEART

OR, THE LIFE-TRIALS OF JESSIE LORING

T. S. ARTHUR

1st WORLD
LIBRARY
Literary Society

The Hand But Not the Heart

T.S. Arthur

© 1st World Library, 2006
PO Box 2211
Fairfield, IA 52556
www.1stworldlibrary.com
First Edition

LCCN: 2006907741

Softcover ISBN: 1-4218-2453-1
Hardcover ISBN: 1-4218-2353-5
eBook ISBN: 1-4218-2553-8

Purchase *"The Hand But Not the Heart"*
as a traditional bound book at:
www.1stWorldLibrary.com/purchase.asp?ISBN=1-4218-2453-1

1st World Library is a literary, educational organization
dedicated to:

- Creating a free internet library of downloadable ebooks

- Hosting writing competitions and offering book
  publishing scholarships.

Interested in more 1st World Library books?
contact: literacy@1stworldlibrary.com
Check us out at: www.1stworldlibrary.com

OUR

ELIZABETH

A Humour Novel

FLORENCE A. KILPATRICK

1st WORLD
LIBRARY
Literary Society

Our Elizabeth

Florence A. Kilpatrick

© 1st World Library, 2006
PO Box 2211
Fairfield, IA 52556
www.1stworldlibrary.com
First Edition

LCCN: 2006907679

Softcover ISBN: 1-4218-2424-8
Hardcover ISBN: 1-4218-2324-1
eBook ISBN: 1-4218-2524-4

Purchase *"Our Elizabeth"*
as a traditional bound book at:
www.1stWorldLibrary.com/purchase.asp?ISBN=1-4218-2424-8

1st World Library is a literary, educational organization
dedicated to:

- Creating a free internet library of downloadable ebooks

- Hosting writing competitions and offering book
  publishing scholarships.

Interested in more 1st World Library books?
contact: literacy@1stworldlibrary.com
Check us out at: www.1stworldlibrary.com

1st World Library Literary Society

Giving Back to the World

"If you want to work on the core problem, it's early school literacy."

- James Barksdale, former CEO of Netscape

"No skill is more crucial to the future of a child, or to a democratic and prosperous society, than literacy."

- Los Angeles Times

Literacy... means far more than learning how to read and write... The aim is to transmit... knowledge and promote social participation."

- UNESCO

"Literacy is not a luxury, it is a right and a responsibility. If our world is to meet the challenges of the twenty-first century we must harness the energy and creativity of all our citizens."

- President Bill Clinton

"Parents should be encouraged to read to their children, and teachers should be equipped with all available techniques for teaching literacy, so the varying needs and capacities of individual kids can be taken into account."

- Hugh Mackay

TO CIS

AUTHOR'S NOTE

Elizabeth is not a type; she is an individuality. Signs and omens at her birth no doubt determined her sense of the superstitious; but I trace her evolution as a figure of fun to some sketches of mine in the pages of Punch. These, however, were only impressions of Elizabeth on a small scale, but I acknowledge the use of them here in the process of developing her to full life-size. Elizabeth, as I say, is a personality apart; there is only one Elizabeth. Here she is.

F. A. K.

CHAPTER I

If you ask Henry he will tell you that I cannot cook. In fact, he will tell you even if you don't ask. To hold up my culinary failures to ridicule is one of his newest forms of humour (new to Henry, I mean - the actual jokes you will have learned already at your grandmother's knee).

I had begun to see that I must either get a servant soon or a judicial separation from Henry. That was the stage at which I had arrived. Things were getting beyond me. By 'things' I mean the whole loathsome business of housework. My *metier* is to write - not that I am a great writer as yet, though I hope to be some day. What I never hope to be is a culinary expert. Should you command your cook to turn out a short story she could not suffer more in the agonies of composition than I do in making a simple Yorkshire pudding.

Henry does not like housework any more than I do; he says the performance of menial duties crushes his spirit - but he makes such a fuss about things. You might think, to hear him talk, that getting up coal, lighting fires, chopping wood and cleaning flues, knives and brasses were the entire work of a household instead of being mere incidents in the daily routine. If he had had to tackle my duties . . . but men never understand how much there is to do in a house.

Even when they do lend a hand my experience is that they invariably manage to hurt themselves in some way. Henry seems incapable of getting up coal without dropping the largest knob on his foot. If he chops wood he gashes himself; he cannot go through the simple rite of pouring boiling water out of a saucepan without getting scalded; and when he mounts the steps to adjust the blinds I always keep the brandy uncorked in readiness; you see, he declares that a chap needs something to pull himself together after a fall from a step-ladder.

Perhaps you trace in all this a certain bitterness, a veiled antagonism on my part towards Henry; you may even imagine that we are a bickering sort of couple, constantly trying to get the better of each other. If so, you are mistaken. Up to six months before this story opens our married life had been ideal - for which reason I didn't open the story earlier. Ideal marriages (to any one except the contracting parties) are uninteresting affairs. It is such a pity that the good, the laudable, things in life generally are.

One of the reasons why our union was ideal (up to six months before this story opens) was that we shared identical tastes. Comradeship is the true basis of - but perhaps you have read my articles on the subject on the Woman's Page of the *Daily Trail*. I always advise girls to marry men of their own temperament. As a matter of fact, I expect they marry the men who are easiest to land, but you're not allowed to say things like that (on the Woman's Page). We have pure and noble ideals, we are tender, motherly and housewifely (on the Woman's Page).

Henry and I were of the same temperament. For one thing, we were equally incompetent at golf. Perhaps I foozled my drive rather worse than Henry, but then he never took fewer than five strokes on the green, whereas I have occasionally done it in four. Then we mutually detested gramophones. But when we discovered that we could both play 'Caller Herrin" on the piano with one finger (entirely by ear) we felt that we were affinities, and got married shortly afterwards.

Stevenson once said, 'Marriage is not a bed of roses; it is a field

Florence A. Kilpatrick

of battle.' At the epoch of which I write Henry and I had not got to turning machine-guns on each other. At the most we only had diplomatic unpleasantnesses. The position, however, was getting strained. I realized quite clearly that if we didn't obtain domestic help of some sort very soon it might come to open hostilities. Isn't it surprising how the petty annoyances of life can wear away the strong bulwarks of trust and friendship formed by years of understanding? Our particular bulwarks were becoming quite shaky through nothing else but having to muddle through the dull sordid grind of cooking and housework by ourselves. We were getting disillusioned with each other. No 'jaundiced eye that casts discolouration' could look more jaundiced than Henry's when I asked him to dry up the dinner things.

Having explained all this, you will now understand something of my feelings when, on going to answer a knock at the door, I was confronted by a solid female who said she had been sent from the Registry Office. Oh, thrice blessed Registry Office that had answered my call.

'Come in,' I said eagerly, and, leading the way into the dining-room, I seated myself before her. With lowered eyes and modest mien I was, of course, waiting for her to speak first. I did not wait long. Her voice, concise and direct, rapped out: 'So you require a cook-general?'

'Yes - er - please,' I murmured. Under her searching gaze my knees trembled, my pulses throbbed, a slight perspiration broke out on my forehead. My whole being seemed to centre itself in the mute inquiry: 'Shall I suit?'

There was a pause while the applicant placed her heavy guns. Then she opened fire immediately. 'I suppose you have outside daily help?'

'Er - no,' I confessed.

'Then you have a boy to do the windows, knives and boots?'

'No.'

'Do you send everything to the laundry?'

'Well . . . no . . . not quite.' I wanted to explain, to modify, to speak airily of woollens being 'just rubbed through,' but she hurried me forward.

'Have you a hot water circulator?'

'No.'

'A gas cooking-range?'

'No.'

It was terrible. I seemed to have nothing. I stood, as it were, naked to the world, bereft of a single inducement to hold out to the girl.

'Do you dine late?'

At this point, when I longed to answer 'No,' I was compelled to say 'Yes.' That decided her. She rose at once and moved towards the door. 'I'm afraid your situation won't do for me,' she remarked.

That was all she said. She was perfectly dignified about it. Much as she obviously condemned me, there was no noisy recrimination, no violent vituperative outburst on her part. I followed in her wake to the door. Even at the eleventh hour I hoped for a respite. 'Couldn't something be arranged?' I faltered as my gaze wandered hungrily over her capable-looking form. 'We might get you a gas-cooker - and all that.'

Do not condemn me. Remember that my will had been weakened by housework; six months of doing my own washing-up had brought me to my knees. I was ready to agree to any terms that were offered me. The applicant shook her head. There were too many obstacles in the way, too many radical changes necessary before the place could be made suitable for her. I realized finality in her answer, 'No, nothink,' and closing the front door behind her, I returned to the study to brood. I was still there, thinking bitterly, the shadows of the evening creeping around me, when Henry came in.

'Hallo,' he said gruffly. 'No signs of dinner yet? Do you know the time?'

And only six months ago (before this story opens) he would have embraced me tenderly when he came in and said, 'How is the little wifie-pifie to-night? I hope it hasn't been worrying its fluffy little head with writing and making its hubby-wubby anxious?'

Perhaps you prefer Henry in the former role. Frankly, I did not. 'You needn't be so impatient,' I retorted. 'I expect you've gorged yourself on a good lunch in town. Anyhow, it won't take long to get dinner, as we're having tinned soup and eggs.'

'Oh, damn eggs,' said Henry. 'I'm sick of the sight of 'em.'

You can see for yourself how unrestrained we were getting. The thin veneer of civilization (thinner than ever when Henry is hungry) was fast wearing into holes. There was a pause, and then I coldly remarked: 'You didn't kiss me when you came in.'

It was a custom to which I was determined to cling with grim resolution. If I allowed his treatment of me to become too casual we might continue to drift apart even when we had some one to do the washing-up.

Henry came over to me and bestowed a labial salute. It is the only adequate description I can give of the performance. Then I went to the kitchen and got out the cookery-book.

It is a remarkable thing that I am never able to cook anything without the aid of the book. Even if I prepare the same dish seven times a week I must have the printed instructions constantly before me, or I am lost. This is especially strange, because I have a retentive memory for other things. My mind is crammed with odd facts retained from casual reading. If you asked me, the date of the Tai-ping Rebellion (though you're not likely to) I could tell you at once that it originated in 1850 and was not suppressed until 1864, for I remember reading about it in a dentist's waiting-room when I was fifteen. Yet although I prepared scrambled eggs one hundred times in six months (Henry said it was much oftener than that) I had to pore over the instructions as earnestly when doing my 'century' as on the first occasion.

The subsequent meal was taken in silence. The hay-fever from which I am prone to suffer at all seasons of the year was particularly persistent that evening. A rising irritability, engendered by leathery eggs and fostered by Henry's expression, was taking possession of me. Quite suddenly I discovered that the way he held his knife annoyed me. Further, his manner of eating soup maddened me. But I restrained myself. I merely remarked: 'You have finished your soup, I *hear*, love.' We had not yet reached the stage of open rupture when I could exclaim: 'For goodness' sake stop swilling down soup like a grampus!' I have never heard a grampus take soup. But the expression seems picturesque.

Henry, too, had not quite lost his fortitude. My hay-fever was obviously annoying him, but he only commented: 'Don't you think you ought to go to a doctor - a really reliable man - with that distressing nasal complaint of yours, my dear?' I knew, however, that he was longing to bark out: 'Can't you do something to stop that everlasting sniffing? It's driving me mad, woman.'

How long would it be before we reached this stage of debacle? I brooded. Then the front door bell rang.

'You go,' I said to Henry.

Florence A. Kilpatrick

'No, you go,' he replied. 'It looks bad for a man if he is master of the house to answer the door.'

I do not know why it should look bad for a man to answer his own door unless he is a bad man. But there are some things in our English social system which will ever remain unquestioned. I rose and went to open the front door. The light from the hall lamp fell dimly on a lank female form which stood on the doorstep. Out of the dusk a voice spoke to me. It said, 'I think you're wantin' a cook-general?'

I cried out in a loud voice, saying, 'I am.'

'Well, I'm Elizabeth Renshaw. You wrote to me. I got your letter sent on from the Registry Office along with ninety others. But I liked yours the best, so I thought there'd be no 'arm in coming to see -'

'Come in, Elizabeth,' I said earnestly. 'I'm glad you liked my letter.'

I began to wonder if I was not a great writer after all.

CHAPTER II

I piloted Elizabeth in and bade her be seated. Strangely enough, my usual hopeful expectations entirely deserted me at that moment. I felt that the interview would be fruitless. They say hope springs eternal in the human breast, but my breast didn't feel human just then. It was throbbing with savage and sanguinary thoughts. Perhaps it was the eggs. Many animals are rendered ferocious by an over-diet of meat. I can testify (so can Henry) that an over-diet of eggs has exactly the same effect on human beings. I think they stimulate the wrong kind of phagocytes. They can make the mildest and most forgiving person wild and vindictive. Henry always declares, when he reads of a man murdering his wife under exceptionally brutal circumstances, that she must have been giving him too many scrambled eggs. In fact, he wrote articles about it, entitled 'The Psychology of Diet,' in the Sunday papers, signed 'By a Physician.'

Henry is not a physician. Neither is he 'An Eminent Surgeon,' 'A Harley Street Expert,' an 'Ex-M.P.,' 'A Special Crime Investigator,' or 'A Well-known Bishop,' although he has written under all these pseudonyms. Do not blame Henry. In private life he seeks the truth as one who seeks the light, but by profession he is a journalist. Not being an expert in anything, he can write about everything - which is the true test of the born journalist.

But to return to Elizabeth. With the remembrance of the similar interview of only a few hours before still rankling in my

Florence A. Kilpatrick

mind, I looked at her a little austerely. This time it was I who began the causerie.

'First of all I must tell you,' I said, 'that we have no hot water circulator.'

'Carn't abide them things,' commented Elizabeth; 'they bust sometimes and blows folks up.'

'We have no outside help,' I continued.

'An' a good thing, too. One place I was in the char 'elped 'erself to things an' it was me who was blamed fer it.'

'We have no gas-cooker.'

'Well, that's all right, then. Don't understand 'em. Give me a proper kitchen range, that's all I ask.'

I looked up hopefully. If all she asked for was a kitchen range I should be glad enough to give her a little thing like that. But the supreme test was yet to come. 'We don't send everything to the laundry,' I began.

'I 'ope you don't,' she broke in, 'leastways my clothes. The state they send 'em back, 'arf torn to ribbons. A girl never 'as 'er 'and out of 'er pocket buying new things. Besides, I like a bit o' washin' - makes a change, I always say.'

My heart began to beat so loudly with hope that I could hardly hear my own voice as I asked, 'How . . . how soon can you come?'

'To-morrow, if you like,' she answered casually. 'I've 'ad a row with the friend I'm stayin' with and I can't abide living-in with folks I've fallen out with.'

I struggled to reconstruct this sentence and then, remembering what was required of me, I remarked, 'And your references?'

She gave me the address of her last place.

'Are they on the 'phone?' I questioned eagerly. 'If so, I'll settle the thing at once.' It seemed they were. I tottered to the telephone. My call was answered by a woman with a thin, sharp voice.

'I am sorry,' she said in answer to my query, 'I must refuse to answer any questions concerning Elizabeth Renshaw.'

'But you only need say "yes" or "no." Is she honest?'

'I am not in a position to give you a reply.'

'Am I to understand that she isn't sober?'

'I cannot answer that question.'

'Look here, she hasn't murdered any one, has she?'

'I am not in a position -'

'Oh, hang the woman,' I muttered, jerking up the receiver. But I felt the situation was an awkward one. What sinister and turbid happenings were connected with Elizabeth and her last place? I meditated. If she were not sober it was, after all, no business of mine so long as she got through her work. And if she didn't we should be no worse off than we were at present.

If she were dishonest it might be awkward, certainly, but then there was nothing of very much value in the house, Henry and I merely being writers by profession. Most of our friends are writers, too, so we have not the usual array of massive silver wedding gifts about the place, but quite a lot of autograph photos and books instead. The value of these might not be apparent to the casual pilferer. My meditations got no further. I decided to lock up my silk stockings and best handkerchiefs and engage Elizabeth without delay. As a matter of fact, I afterwards discovered that her career had been blameless, while she had every foundation for her favourite declaration, 'I wouldn't take a used postage stamp, no, nor a rusty nail that wasn't my own.'

I do not condemn the woman I interviewed on the telephone, reprehensible as was her conduct. Perhaps she, too, was living on eggs and it had warped her better nature.

'I suppose you can cook all right?' I asked Elizabeth as ten minutes later, all arrangements made, I accompanied her to the door.

'Me? I'm a rare 'and at cookin'. My friend's 'usband ses 'e's never come across any one who can cook a steak like I can.'

'A steak,' I murmured ecstatically, 'richly brown with softly swelling curves -'

'Rather underdone in the middle,' supplemented Elizabeth, 'just a little bit o' fat, fairly crisp, a lump o' butter on the top, and I always 'old that a dash o' fried onion improves the flavour.'

'How beautiful,' I murmured again. It sounded like a poem. Swinburne or de Musset have never stirred me so deeply as did that simple recitation.

Elizabeth, seeing that she had an attentive audience, continued, 'Take roast pork, now. Well, I always say there's a lot in the cookin' o' that, with crisp cracklin', apple sauce an' stuffin' -'

'Don't go on,' I, broke in, feeling in my weakened state, unable to stand any more. Tears that men weep had risen to my eyes. 'Promise,' I said, taking her toil-worn hand, 'that you will come to-morrow.'

'Right-o,' said Elizabeth, and her lank form disappeared in the darkness. I staggered into the dining-room. Henry was sitting at the disordered dinner table jotting down notes. At any other time this would have irritated me, because I knew it was a preliminary to his remark that as he had an article to write which must be finished that evening he would not be able to help me with the washing-up. A hackneyed dodge of his. Oh, I could tell you a tale of the meanness of men.

'Henry, something has happened,' I began.

Without looking round he remarked, 'Don't disturb me. I must write up a brief biographical sketch of Courtenay Colville, the actor. He's been taken seriously ill and may be dead just in time for the morning papers.' In this way do journalists speak. To them life and death, all the tremendous happenings of the world - wars, revolutions, or even weddings of revue actresses - are just so much matter for printed and pictorial display. Do you think, if a great and honoured statesman dies, sub-editors care two pins about his public services? Not they. All they worry about is whether he is worth double-column headings, a long primer intro., and a line across the page.

'I didn't know Courtenay Colville was so ill,' I commented mildly. What I did know was that he was reported to have sprained his right toe at golf, and only an hour previously I should have commented caustically on Henry's description of this 'serious illness.' Now I came up to him and put my arm about his neck.

'I've just put on a clean collar - be careful,' he said, shaking off my hand.

'Henry, dear, I've landed a servant at last,' I breathed.

He looked up and, for a moment, I felt that I ought not to have told him so suddenly. But joy does not often kill. I went and knelt beside him. 'Dearest,' I whispered, 'it seems as though all the bitterness and misunderstanding between you and me is to be swept away at last. She can cook steaks, dear -

juicy steaks, pork with crackling -'

'Sage and onion stuffing?' burst in a hoarse murmur from Henry.

'Yes, and large mutton chops, rich in fat -'

'Dearest, how splendid,' whispered Henry. Our lips met in ecstacy.

That evening was one of the happiest we have ever spent. Henry and I sat together on the divan and looked at the cookery-book. There was no doubt about it. Henry said, that Mrs. Beeton was a wonderful woman. We felt that she and Mr. Beeton must have been tremendously happy in their married life.

The illustrations to the book delighted us, too, with their bold outlines, vigorous colouring, and, attention to detail. Henry and I rather favour the impressionist school in art, but when you're admiring a picture of salmon mayonnaise it refreshes you to distinguish the ingredients.

Elizabeth arrived the next day, bringing with her a small - perplexingly small - brown paper parcel. The rest of her luggage, she said, was on the way. It remained on the way so long that I finally got uneasy and began to question her about it. She did not seem so disturbed at the prospect of its being lost as I did. At last, when I declared my intention of writing Carter Paterson's about it on her behalf, she confessed. Frankness is one of her distinguishing qualities.

'My box is still at my friend's,' she explained. 'You see, when I goes to a new place I never 'ave my luggage sent on until I feel I'm going to settle. It saves a lot o' bother - if I don't stop.'

'I hadn't thought of that,' I commented feebly.

'I brought a clean cap and another pair o' stockings with me, so I'm all right for a fortnight,' she went on. Her creed, like her change of underclothing, was obviously simple. Mournfully I withdrew from the kitchen to meditate.

So we were on probation. It was a tremulous time. I bade Henry tread softly and not to forget to rub his feet on the mat. I gave all my orders to Elizabeth in a voice which blended deference with supplication. I strove hard to live up to what I thought must be her conception of the Perfect Mistress. And when, the fortnight expired, Carter Paterson drove up and deposited a small corded box on the hall mat, I felt it to be a personal triumph. But Henry said I had nothing to do with it. To this day he declares that Elizabeth decided to stop because she so earnestly desired to serve such a gentle master.

CHAPTER III

No doubt you will have guessed that Henry is a better and sounder writer than I. He has helped me a lot with his criticism and advice, for he is fastidious regarding style. There used to be a time, before he came along, when I walked in darkness, often beginning sentences with conjunctions and ending them with adverbs; I have even split infinitives and gone on my way rejoicing. I am now greatly improved, though one of the incurable things I shall never eradicate from my system is a weakness for beginning sentences with 'but.' But if you observe it, I hope you will kindly pass it over without remark.

Henry often talks to me about construction. 'If you are writing a book,' he says, 'don't introduce all your characters in the first chapter. Let them develop gradually.'

Now that is sound advice. It was not, however, for the sake of construction that I refrained from telling you about The Kid at the very beginning. I was impelled to silence by the same reason which kept me from mentioning The Kid to Elizabeth until her box had arrived and she had settled down. I feel sure you do not want to hear about The Kid any more than Elizabeth did. It is annoying to read about children. If they are good they cloy, and if bad they irritate. The Kid is neither. In any case, it is time she came home now, so she will have to drop in here. During my servantless period she stayed with friends - which was a good thing for her digestion and my nervous system. Now there was no longer any excuse - I mean, it was now time for her to return.

She is what you would call a boisterous child, overflowing with ebullition of spirits, *joie de vivre*, bonhomie, and all those attributes which cause people possessing them to make a noise. When she enters a room you always think of those lines, 'the mountains skipped like rams, and the little hills like young sheep.'

She descended on Henry and me just a year after our marriage. As we have now been married ten years you will be able to calculate her age if you are good at arithmetic.

Elizabeth did not disapprove of The Kid. It might have been awkward if she had. As a matter of fact, they became close companions at sight. There were certain affinities between them. Elizabeth, for example, although perhaps not so habitually sticky as The Kid, like her didn't seem able to remain clean or tidy for longer than half an hour at a time. Also, Elizabeth believing in Signs, The Kid revered her for her mysticism - about the only person who ever did. She used to beg to be allowed to study her Dream Book, and every evening before bedtime would go into the kitchen and - sitting amid that wild disorder that is necessary to Elizabeth before she can really feel at home - 'look up' her dream of the previous night.

Try as she would, the poor child never seemed to have the sort of vision that, in the words of the book, had 'excellent portent.' 'I don't get the nice things,' I once heard her remark, 'like white horses, you know, which, it says, portend honours, riches and rare gifts. Did you ever dream of white horses, Elizabeth?'

'That I did - wunst.'

'And did you get the honours, and all those things, Elizabeth?'

'Well, I got the rare gifts in a manner o' speaking. My gran'mother died a month later an' left me a pair o' jet earrings

Florence A. Kilpatrick

and a jet bracelet to match - one o' them stretchin' ones, on elastic, you know.'

That incident established Elizabeth in The Kid's estimation as a prophet. Old Moore himself couldn't have done better.

I did not pay much attention to these things; and it was not until Elizabeth had been with me for some time that I discovered her intense fatalism. She ordered her life by Signs, in fact. You or I might drop a tablespoon on the floor and think nothing of it, but she would tell you at once it was a Sign that a tall dark lady was coming to the house. If a knife fell you would hear her mutter *'That's* a man.' According to Elizabeth, success in life is in no wise due to personal effort - it all depends on whether you are 'born lucky.'

Unfortunately Elizabeth was 'born unlucky' - unfortunately for me as well as her. Destiny, having now woven my life with hers, it made me unlucky, too. For example, she would come to me and announce, 'I've been unlucky an' broke the teapot this mornin'. That means I'll break another two things afore the week's out. It always goes in threes.'

'Then hadn't you better smash something that is of no value at once,' was my obvious suggestion, 'and get it over?'

But Elizabeth, entrenched in her convictions, would shake her head. 'That's no good. I've tried that afore an' it didn't work. You see, it 'as to be done unexpected to break the spell.' So the spell had to be broken also. Clearly, human intervention was no good at all. Fate was against both of us.

There is something positively uncanny in the way misfortune lies in wait for that girl. You would think that after causing her to break two full breakfast services it would leave her alone for a while. But no; she was half-way through the third before her luck showed any signs of changing.

Spilling the salt accounted for three burnt saucepans and the collapse of the plate rack (at the moment fully charged); while seeing the new moon through glass caused her to overlook the fact that she had left a can in the middle of the staircase. Afterwards (during the week that I waited on her on account of her sprained ankle) she said she would never go near a window again until the moon was at full and quite safe.

Of course, I do my best to parry these mysterious blows of Fate. I remember when she first undertook to clean the drawing-room I took away everything that a mysterious agency might cause to 'come in two' in her hands. I left her alone with the grand piano and scrubbing materials, and went out to spend the afternoon with cheerful countenance. I returned rather late, and directly Elizabeth opened the door to me I saw that something was wrong.

'I've been unlucky,' she began.

'Unlucky!' I faltered. 'But what with? Don't say the piano came in two in your hands?'

'It wasn't my 'ands, it was my feet. The floor gave way an' I went through.'

'You went through the floor!' I marvelled. Then my face cleared. The house was not mine, and, after all, the landlord has no right to escape these unusual machinations of Fate.

'I knew somethink would 'appen when I put the boots on the table by accident this mornin',' she explained, 'It's always a Bad Sign.'

You must not think, however, that Elizabeth ever allows her fatalism to interfere with her judgment. I recall the occasion when she came to me looking actually concerned and remarked: 'I'm sorry, 'm, but them two varses that was on the mantelpiece in the pink bedroom -'

I started up. 'Don't dare to say you've been unlucky with them!'

'No'm, I wasn't unlucky. I was just careless when I broke those.'

A low moan escaped my lips. They were the Sevres vases that I loved dearest of my possessions, and which, in the words of those who keep shops, 'cannot be repeated.' I regarded Elizabeth angrily, no longer able to control my wrath. I am at times (says Henry) a hasty woman. I ought to have paused and put my love of Sevres vases in the balance with the diet of scrambled eggs and the prospect of unlimited washing-up, and I know which side would have tipped up at once. However, I did not pause, caring not that the bitter recriminations I intended to hurl at her would bring forth the inevitable month's notice; that, at the first hint of her leaving me, at least a dozen of my neighbours would stretch out eager hands to snatch Elizabeth, a dozen different vacant sinks were ready for her selection. I did not care, I say; I had loved my vases and in that moment I hated Elizabeth.

But she began to speak before I did. 'It isn't as if I'd been unlucky - I couldn't ha' 'elped *that*. But I know when I'm in the wrong' - she unfolded a parcel she had in her hand as she spoke - 'so I went out larst night and bought these to replace what I broke. Right's right, I always say'; and she laid down before me a pair of vases on which were emblazoned gigantic and strangely-hued flowers that could belong to no earthly flora.

'They're bigger'n the varses I broke,' she murmured, regarding her purchase with satisfaction.

Then I noted that she wore an expression of lofty pride, that she glowed with the calm satisfaction of one who has made ample reparation. Looking at Elizabeth just then you might almost have thought that she had a soul. Really, it gave one an odd feeling.

I picked up her offering and regarded it a moment in silence, while my aesthetic nature shook to its foundations. Stifling the moan of horror that had risen to my lips, I faced her with a smile. Balaclava heroes could have done no more.

'Thank you, Elizabeth,' I said humbly.

CHAPTER IV

Marion often says that if Elizabeth hadn't . . . but I believe I haven't told you about Marion yet. I'm afraid I shall never learn construction, in spite of Henry.

Well, Marion is Henry's sister. She is what you would call a really nice girl. Everybody likes her and sends for her when in trouble or needing advice. Women adore her and tell her all their secrets, and get her to alter their dresses for them. Men seek her company in order to pour out their worries and anxieties into her sympathetic ear. She is always acting as intermediary in love affairs that are not running smoothly and need the intervention or assistance of a third party. But - and this is where the poignant touch comes in - she never had a love affair of her own. I could not understand why. It isn't that she's unattractive, being quite pretty in that feminine clinging way which we generally connect with the Victorian era.

There is a certain type of man who admires this type of woman. He writes to the newspapers, clamouring loudly to be told where the 'nice' girls are (the girls of modest mien who know only the gentle, housewifely arts), and signs himself 'Old-Fashioned' or 'Early Victorian,' or merely gives baffling initials, always being careful not to disclose his identity. If he really wants these sort of girls why doesn't he give a name and address to which they can be forwarded?

It is my belief that men like these 'nice' homely women as mothers, but do not seek for them as wives. But, I ask, how are they to be mothers - and still remain 'nice' - if they are not first to be selected as wives? If the position isn't faced they will soon die out altogether and become as rare as the brontosaurus. We shall go to museums and see exhibited, 'Fossilized remains of "Nice Girl": supposed to exist in early part of twentieth century. Rare specimen.'

Everybody said Marion ought to be married as she had those fine qualities which belong to the ideal home-maker. Nearly every man who knew her declared that she would make a perfect wife - and then went off and married someone else. They said the chap would be lucky who got her - which was true enough - but the idea of going in to win her didn't seem to occur to any one of them.

So here was Marion, sweet and lovable, who would make a delightful mother of children and of a home a haven of refuge, languishing alone for want of a suitable offer of marriage.

I will frankly admit that I planned various matrimonial schemes for Marion. Many eligible men did I invite to meet her; some fell on stony ground, and others made excuses and stayed away.

I remained undaunted, although I got no assistance from Henry, who strongly disapproved of my manoeuvres. In any case, he would never have been of much help in the matter, being quite unable to distinguish between the Right and the Wrong kind of man. Also, nearly all his friends are either married with grown-up children, or elderly widowers with hearts so firmly embedded in the graves of their former wives that it would be perfectly impossible to try to excavate them again.

The annoying thing about Henry, too, is his lack of discernment regarding men. I have known him speak glowingly, and with unabated enthusiasm, of 'a most interesting chap' he has met at his club, referring to him as 'altogether delightful,' 'a charming conversationalist,' and so on, until I have felt impelled to ask Henry to bring this treasure home to dinner.

Then, after expending myself in the preparation of such things as *hors d'oeuvres* and iced cocktails and putting on my most becoming frock Henry has walked in with a veritable monster of a man. You know the kind I mean. Quite good and God-fearing and all that, but with one of those dreadful clematis moustaches which cling half over the face, beginning at the nostrils and curling under the chin, a form which undulates in the region of the waistcoat, and a slow and pompous conversation (mainly devoted to the discussion of politics in the 'fifties).

I remember, shortly after one of these visitations, Henry ringing me up on the 'phone and asking if it was convenient to bring a man home to dinner that evening.

'What is he like?' I inquired, still smarting under recent experiences, 'has he much moustache - I mean, is he nice?'

Henry paused. 'Oh, all right. I don't know whether you'd care for him. Perhaps I'd better not -'

'Yes, bring him if you want to, dear,' I conceded. I am not one of those fussy wives. I like Henry to feel that he can bring a friend home whenever he likes; but on this occasion I did not make unusual preparations. After bidding Elizabeth turn the cold meat into curry and judiciously water the soup to make it enough for four instead of three, I tidied my hair and descended into the hall to see Henry helping a man off with his overcoat - and such a man! It was the dashing, the handsome, the witty Harvey Trevor (political writer on the *Morning Sun*).

It was too late to back upstairs again and improvise upon my toilette, for they both looked up and saw me at that moment. So there I stood, like a stag at bay, with my nose unpowdered (Henry would say that a stag doesn't powder its nose, but you will know what I mean) wearing my dullest and most uninspired house-frock, and hurling silent anathemas at my heartless husband.

You will now understand how useless Henry was as an ally in my matrimonial plans for Marion. But I was doggedly determined that she should make some man happy. At last, indeed, it seemed as though my efforts were to be crowned with success when George Harbinger appeared on the scene.

He took to her at once and said that she was just the sort of girl his mother would like. He declared that Marion's oyster patties were things of pure delight and ought to be eaten to slow music. (Yes, I always got Marion to make some of her special pastry when the eligibles came to dine.) He openly sought her society. They even played draughts together and he always won. Everything was going splendidly.

I was especially satisfied, for George Harbinger was an estimable man. He was an assessor, and entirely reliable. Indeed, I believe it would be difficult to find an assessor who is not. When you read the police court cases you find all sorts of professions and followings represented in the charge sheets, from actors down to editors, but have you ever heard of an assessor who defaulted, who committed bigamy, arson, larceny, murder, or neglected to pay his income tax? No, you have not. Also, you seldom hear of an unmarried assessor. They are known to be such steady, dependable men that they are always snapped up at once. Thus you can understand how pleased I was to get hold of George.

One evening it seemed as though things were getting to a climax. George had eaten four of Marion's oyster patties at dinner and, after retaining her hand for an undue length of time at parting, asked if he could see her alone if he called the following evening, as he had something important to say to her.

Marion was in a flutter. She admitted that she 'rather liked' George. (Your nice girl never says outright that she's keen on a man.) 'And what do you think,' she confessed, 'he said when we were playing draughts to-night that I was just the sort of girl his mother would like, and - and -'

'Yes, go on,' I said tensely.

'That he never believed in a man marrying a girl of whom his mother did not approve. What do you think he meant by that, dear?'

'Everything,' I said, and took a silent decision to leave no stone unturned to bring the thing off all right. I planned to leave them alone in the rose drawing-room with its pink-shaded lights - Marion looks her best under pink-shaded lights. She was thirty-seven, but only looked thirty when she had her hair waved and wore her grey *charmeuse*.

I, myself, prepared her for the interview. I dressed her hair becomingly and clasped my matrix necklace around her throat. Then, soon after George arrived, I excused myself on the plea of having an article to write - which was perfect truth - and left them alone together.

Doesn't it give you a feeling of contentment when you have done a good action? You are permeated with a sort of glow which comes from within. After closing the drawing-room door on Marion and George, I sat down to work in an atmosphere of righteousness. I could almost imagine there must be the beginnings of a faint luminous disc around my head.

The subject of the article I now began to write was 'Should Women Propose?' Treading carefully on the delicate ground of the Woman's Page, I decided that they must do nothing that is so utterly unfeminine. 'But there are many subtle little ways in which a woman can convey to a man her preference for him,' I penned, 'without for a moment overstepping the bounds of that maidenly reticence which is one of the charms of -'

The door opened and Elizabeth entered. Elizabeth has a way of entering when I am most likely to lose the thread of my sentence.

'I'm fair worried about Miss Marryun,' she began.

I looked up with a start. 'What on earth do you mean?'

'Well, you see, the Signs are against 'er. They've bin against 'er for days. Yesterday I see 'er sneeze three times to the left, an' that's bad. Then when she put her right shoe on 'er wrong foot by accident, I felt somethin' was comin'. But after I found two triangles an' a mouse in 'er cup to-day I knew -'

'A mouse in her cup!' I marvelled.

'Fortune tellin' by tea-leaves, 'm. Well, a mouse is a Bad Sign. It's my belief that she won't get no propogal this evenin'.'

I looked at Elizabeth sternly. I do not wish to insinuate for one moment that she is in the habit of listening at doors, but she certainly gains an insight into our private lives that is nothing short of uncanny.

'I just been lookin' at the cards,' she continued, 'an' they say as plain as can be that Mr. 'Arbinger isn't the one. 'E's the wrong colour.'

'And what colour do you expect him to be?' I demanded.

''Im bein' fair takes King o' Dimonds. Well, Queen o' Clubs - that's Miss Marryun - is seven cards removed from 'im and the three o' spades comin' between spells disappointment. But, as I ses to 'er quite recent, I ses, "If you want to see your true love aright go into the garding by pale moonlight, walk in a circle, and say, -

  "If I my true love now would see -"'

Florence A. Kilpatrick

'Elizabeth,' I broke in, 'don't forget to grill master's bloaters for breakfast.' In this way do I recall her and remind her of her duty when she ignores the chasms of caste and class distinction which yawn between us.

'Grilled, 'm? Right-o. Well, as I was sayin' about Miss Marryun. She's gotta ring in 'er fortune and she *will* get married, but it will be to a dark man who'll cross water to meet her. She's like me. She isn't fated to meet the right one yet.'

This was a subtle reference to her own chaotic love affairs. Elizabeth never has any lack of young men.' But they are like ships that pass in the night (her night out as a rule), and one by one they drift off, never stopping to cast anchor in her vicinity. You know what I mean. Elizabeth can't keep her young men. They seem attracted to her at first, but, as I say, after a very short time they drift.

'We shall see wot we shall see,' went on Elizabeth, 'there aint no knowin' an' there aint no tellin'. But wot I ses is, if this 'ere propogal don't come orf this evenin', I gotta plan. Of course, one marries accordin' to Fate, but sometimes it doesn't do no 'arm to give Fate an 'elpin' 'and, like.'

Nodding darkly, she melted out. I did not at the time attach any significance to her final words. How was I to guess at those schemes which were even then fermenting in her mind and ended by involving not only Marion and Another, but the entire family?

CHAPTER V

Marion gave me what the newspapers term 'a verbatim report' of the interview which took place between her and George Harbinger. She omitted no detail. As far as I understand, when I left them he was standing with his right foot on the fender and the other on the rug, and his elbow on the mantelpiece. She was sitting in the easy chair to the left of the fireplace, in the full glow of the shaded lamp, knitting a jumper. There was a pause and then he began, 'You never seem idle for a minute. How nimble your fingers are!'

Marion knitted a little harder.

'I have always hoped,' he went on, 'that the woman I married would be fond of her needle. There is something so restful in the idea of coming home in the evening to see one's companion sitting at the fireside engaged in such womanly tasks.'

Marion said that, no doubt, after a hard day at assessing, such a sight would be soothing to a man.

He now came and sat beside her. 'I want to ask you something rather important,' he said, 'but I wonder if I have known you long enough to warrant it.'

She paused in her knitting for a moment to remind him - very earnestly - that real friendship and understanding is more a matter of affinity than actual length of acquaintance.

Florence A. Kilpatrick

'You're right,' he said, pondering, 'and, of course, you're so . . . so sensible.'

Women hate to be told they are sensible by any one but their mothers-in-law. But how could an assessor know that? He continued to regard her earnestly. 'I feel sure, too, that you're so much older than you look.'

To this day Marion says she's not sure whether this was intended as a compliment or a deadly insult.

'Do you think,' he went on, 'that a man should ask a woman to marry him only when she has reached maturity?'

Marion, moving well into the glow of the pink-shaded lamp, said it depended on the stage of maturity. Nowadays, when women so often look younger than they really are, it is difficult to tell.

He seemed relieved. 'That's exactly what I feel about it. But supposing my mother shouldn't approve of my choice? I hate family squabbles above everything. I have always maintained that I would only marry the woman that my mother really liked.'

'Isn't that rather a handicap for your future wife?' asked Marion gently. 'But why not ask your mother's opinion of her?'

'That's just what I want to speak to you about,' he put in eagerly. 'I . . . I want to ask you if I can introduce you to my mother?'

The knitting fell from Marion's nerveless fingers. She can show you the uneven row on the jumper where she dropped fifteen stitches at that moment.

'I shall be most happy to meet your mother,' she murmured.

'This is really good of you,' he said eagerly. 'You see, you're the very one she would take to in an instant. I knew it directly I met you. I don't know any one else she would listen to so willingly, if you will consent to intervene.'

'Intervene!' echoed Marion. Somehow she did not like the word. Not at that moment, I mean.

'Yes, intervene,' he repeated. There was no mistaking it - what could be clearer. Latin, *inter*, between; *venio*, I come. Marion may have translated it differently, but she had served in the capacity of buffer too often to misinterpret its meaning.

'I am to understand that you wish for my aid in a love affair?' she said.

'That's just about it. You see, I always hoped I should fall in love with a quiet, homely, staid sort of girl, but dash it all, you can't govern these things, can you?'

'Sometimes one has to,' said Marion, picking up dropped stitches.

'So I've completely lost my heart to a girl who - well, she's an actress. She's second from the left in the front row chorus of "Whizz-Bang" at the Hilarity Theatre; I tell you she's wonderful.'

'No doubt,' said Marion, bending lower over her knitting.

'Lottie's quite a good little girl, you know, but she's so young - barely twenty - and she can't cook or sew or housekeep or do any of those things which my mother approves. But she dances wonderfully and kicks higher than anyone else in the chorus -'

'And you want me to make your mother appreciate the . . . the . . . high kicks?' broke in Marion rather bitterly.

'Well, not exactly, but you know what mothers are - about the

Florence A. Kilpatrick

stage, I mean. So don't you understand that if some sensible little woman like you were to speak to her about it, she might reconstruct her views -'

He paused, staring in a puzzled way at Marion. Beneath her gentle exterior she has a decided temper which she is apt to deplore and, she affirms, must instantly be held in check. This, however, was an occasion when she did not seem to think the check action need be applied. She faced George with flashing eyes.

'If you were anything of a man,' she declared, 'you would manage an affair like that alone without asking help from your woman friends. Good evening.'

'Good evening,' responded George, not, I suppose, at the moment thinking of anything more original to say. He departed in a pensive mood.

'And that,' said Marion, concluding the narrative, 'is all there is to be told.'

She sat before me with her eyes downcast, her lips quivering, and a fierce anger rose within me against George Harbinger and mankind in general who could be so blind to Marion's excellent qualities. As I took her in my arms and comforted her, kissing her soft cheeks and fluffy hair, I felt that if I were a man she would be the one woman above all others that I would desire to have and to hold henceforth and for evermore. 'Never mind,' I said tenderly, 'some day you'll meet another who will -'

'No, no, I never shall,' interposed Marion, now openly weeping on my shoulder. 'I shall never interest any one; I know that now. You can't understand, Netta, for men are attracted towards you. If Henry died tomorrow, you'd have half a dozen offers of marriage at once.'

I was rather startled at this suggestion, which somehow hinted disregard for the unconscious Henry.

'I think I must lack charm,' went on Marion in a choked voice. 'Who was it described charm as a - a - sort of a bloom on a woman, and said if she had that she didn't need anything else?'

'It was Barrie,' I said, stroking her hair, 'but don't take any notice of him, dear.'

'It's just what a man would say. Oh, Netta, why is life so hard to a woman? Why must she always be the one to stifle her feelings, repress her natural instincts, wait for man to take the lead? Why can't she be the leading spirit if she wishes, without being humiliated? Why shouldn't women propose?'

'That's just what I've been writing about,' I said involuntarily.

She raised her head from my shoulder. 'And what did you say about it?'

'I held that a woman can - er - oh, hang it all, never mind what I *wrote* about it. What I *say* is that of course they ought to propose if they want to. There should be perfect equality of the sexes.'

'Well, if there was,' put in Marion, her practical common sense coming to her aid, 'it wouldn't after all make a man want to marry me just because it was I who put the question. It's no use, Netta. I'm a born old maid. I've got to go through life heart-hungry, loving other people's babies instead of my own, and stepping aside to let all the fair things go past me.'

Poor little Marion! She looked very wistful and pathetic at that moment. A lump rose in my throat as I strove to dry her eyes and find words of comfort.

She sobbed on unrestrainedly, however, and nothing I could say would soothe her. 'Marion, darling,' I whispered, my own eyes growing moist, 'don't cry any more. Isn't there anything I can say to cheer you up? Can't I suggest anything -?'

The door opened and Elizabeth entered. She carried a tray in her hand on which were a bottle of stout and a glass.

'I thort so,' she said, setting down the tray and looking at Marion's drooping form. 'Ah, these men - 'ounds, I call 'em. I came in to 'ave a word with Miss Marryun and cheer 'er up, like. I bin through it myself, so I knows.'

She approached Marion and laid a damp red hand on her shoulder. 'I bin lookin' at the cards for you, miss, an' I see a loverly future,' she began in a coaxing voice. 'I see a tall dark man crossin' water for you, with a present in 'is right 'and.'

Marion, who was not without a sense of humour, smiled rather wanly. Encouraged, Elizabeth continued: 'Wot's the use o' spoilin' your pretty eyes cryin' for the moon - by which I mean Mr. 'Arbinger - when 'e isn't your Fate? Why, bless you, I was once goin' to marry a plumber's mate, and jest a week afore the weddin 'e went orf with some one else an' owin' me arf-a-crown, too. I was cut up at the time, but I know now 'e wasn't my Fate, 'avin been told since that I'm goin' to marry a man wot'll work with 'is brain. So cheer up, Miss Marryun, and come an' 'ave this nice glarss o' stout I've brought in for you.' She unscrewed the bottle as she spoke. 'I always find that when things are at their worst, an' you're feelin' real pipped like, a glarss o' stout acts like magic. Yes, it's the right stuff, is stout.'

The situation was distinctly ludicrous. Yet neither Marion nor I laughed. We watched Elizabeth solemnly pouring out the stout, after which she handed it to Marion, who, though she 'never touches' anything alcoholic as a rule, took it and drank it off 'like a lamb,' as Elizabeth expressed it.

There was a pause. Then the corners of Marion's mouth ceased to droop. She smiled. I smiled. Elizabeth smiled.

There was another pause. 'I think, Elizabeth,' I remarked, 'I'll have a glass - just a small glass - of stout myself.'

'You do right, 'm. I'll fetch you a glass.'

'And Elizabeth, if you'd care to have some -'

'Thank you very much 'm, I *did* take the liberty of 'avin' a taste already, but a little drop more wouldn't do me any 'arm, as the sayin' is.'

She went out. Marion set down her glass and put away her pocket-handkerchief. 'How silly of me to worry about Mr. Harbinger,' she said. 'After all, I suppose Fate never intended us for each other.'

I recognized in a flash that Elizabeth had succeeded where I had failed, and I was conscious of a certain admiration for her methods. Yet at that moment no hint of subsequent events filtered into my mind; I did not suspect - even dimly - the possibilities of Elizabeth.

Florence A. Kilpatrick

CHAPTER VI

Neither Elizabeth or Marion like William. Of the two, Elizabeth is more tolerant towards him, merely commenting that 'she couldn't abide his ways.' Marion, however, views him with an antipathy entirely foreign to one of her gentle nature. I think, in the light of what happened later, if she had only shown a little more forbearance towards him it might have simplified matters.

William is our friend. He drops in to see us when he likes, sits with his feet on our mantelpiece, strews tobacco ash on the carpet, and always tells me which of my hats are the most unbecoming, so you can imagine what a close friend he is. Though he does not stick any closer than a brother, he is equally as frank. He likes Henry and tolerates me. For the rest of the women in the world he has a strong objection. Not that he is a misogynist; but he always holds that a woman interferes with a man's life. I often think that William would be all the better for a little judicious feminine interference. He has, however, now got beyond the stage of redemption.

Home means nothing more to William than a comfortable ledge below the mantelpiece where he can put his feet, a carpet which will not spoil with tobacco ash, and a few tables and chairs scattered about just to hold a good supply of old magazines and newspapers handy for lighting his pipe. He wears those shaggy, unbrushed-looking clothes which all good women abhor. Worst of all, he is constantly getting imbued with new and fantastic ideas which cause him to live in a (quite unnecessary) ferment of enthusiasm.

A good wife, now, would nip these ideas in the bud and make existence infinitely more restful to him. Henry and he once got up a notion of inventing a new drink which was to make them both everlastingly famous and superlatively rich. They talked about it for hours and had even got to designing the labels and bottles when I stepped in and told Henry not to be a silly ass, that he was making a fool of himself, and a few other sensible wifely things like that which finally brought him to reason. William, however, having no one to bring him to reason, goes on day by day becoming more of a lunatic. I could never understand why there is such a close bond between him and Henry, unless it is because they enjoy arguing together. Henry, being a Scotsm an, likes argument; and William, being an Irishman, likes hearing his own voice. Thus they seldom got bored with each other.

The time we did get bored with William was when he turned inventor. It came rather as a surprise to us; and when he began to be abstracted, profoundly meditative, almost sullen, with an apparent desire to be alone, we thought at first that it was the onset of hydrophobia. In fact, we looked it up on the back of the dog-licence to make sure.

William's remarks next became irrelevant. For example, after being wrapped in silence for over half an hour, he suddenly flung out the question, 'How many people do you know who possess a trousers-press?

Faced with the problem, I confessed I could not connect a single acquaintance with a trousers-press. 'Henry hasn't got one,' I admitted.

'Neither have I,' said William. (I didn't doubt that for an instant.) He went on to remark that he knew many men in many walks of life, and only two of them owned a trousers-press, and they shared it between them. Yet the inventor of this apparently negligible article had made a small fortune out of the idea.

'If,' concluded William, 'you can make a small fortune out of a thing that you can dispense with, how much more can you make out of something that you can't do without?'

This sentence I give as William composed it, and from its construction you will understand the state of his mind, for he was as fastidious regarding style as Henry himself. Of course there was some excuse for him. You see, when you're an inventor you can't be anything else. It takes all your time. Judging by William's procedure you must sit up experimenting all night long; you lie down in your clothes and snatch a little sleep at odd moments. When you walk abroad you stride along muttering, waving your arms and bumping into people; you forget to eat; your friends fall away from you. Let me advise parents who are thinking of a career for their sons never to make inventors of them. It's a dog's life. Far better to put them to something with regular hours, say from 10.30 to 4 o'clock, which leaves them with the evenings free.

William wouldn't divulge what his invention was, because, he said, he was afraid of the idea getting about before he took out the patent. He merely told us it was a device which no man living could do without. But he went so far as to show us the inner workings of his discovery (hereinafter referred to as It), which, not knowing what they were for, rather mystified us. I know there was a small suction valve which involved the use of water, because William demonstrated to us one Sunday afternoon in the drawing-room. He said afterwards that the unexpected deluge that broke over the politely interested faces gathered round him was merely due to a leakage in the valve, and he set to work to repair it at once.

At that time William always carried on his person a strange assortment of screws, metal discs, springs, bits of rubber and the like. He pulled them out in showers when he took out his handkerchief; they dripped from him when he stood up. I think he kept them about him for inspiration.

William completed It in a frenzy of enthusiasm. He said that nothing now stood between him and a vast fortune, and in a mood of reckless generosity he promised us all shares, which certainly tended to deepen our interest in the invention. Then he betook himself to the Patent Office.

I saw him the following day, and it occurred to me at once that all was not well with William. For one thing he did not burst in unannounced with hair dishevelled, which seems to be the usual way for an inventor to come into a room; he entered slowly and sat down heavily.

'Is anything wrong with the invention?' I asked.

He pulled out his handkerchief and mopped his brow. A metal disc fell out and rolled unheeded across the floor.

'Nothing is wrong with it,' he answered dully.

'You don't mean that some one else has thought of It before you?'

'Most people seem to have thought of It.' He paused and absently plucked off a stray piece of rubber from his coat sleeve. 'It seems to have originated in America in 1880. Then a large colony of German inventors applied for the patent; a body of Russians were imbued with the idea; several Scandinavians had variations of it. It even seems to have filtered into the brain of certain West African tribes; and in 1918 a Czecho-Slovak -' He paused, overcome with emotion.

'But if It is a thing man can't do without, why haven't we heard of it?' I demanded.

'Men,' replied William sadly, seem determined to do without It. They don't know what is good for them.'

Suddenly he raised his head with the light of enthusiasm in his eyes. 'By the way, I was talking to a chap at the Patent Office

Florence A. Kilpatrick

who told me that there's an enormous boom in inventing in this country just now. Henry ought to get a good article out of it.'

As a matter of fact it was the only thing that ever was got out of the invention.

William, being an Irishman, didn't let failure depress him in the least. We were all glad to see him rational again - as rational as could be expected from him, I mean. As Elizabeth was wont to express it, "E aint screwed up like other folk, so what can you expect.' But as I have said, she did not approve of William. It was not so much that she took exception to the trail of tobacco ash that followed in his wake, or the unusual litter he created during his inventive period. She resented the fact that he was unmarried, having, at all times, a strong objection to celibacy.

'When a man gets to the age o' that there Mr. Roarings' (William's surname is Rawlings, so she didn't get so far out for her) - 'an' isn't married 'e's cheatin' some pore girl out of 'er rights, I ses,' she declared. 'Selfishness! Spendin' all 'is money on 'isself. W'y isn't 'e married?'

'I don't know, Elizabeth,' I replied, 'but if you like, I'll ask him.'

'That'll do no good. 'E orter be thrown together with the right kind o' young lady and kept up to the scratch. That's wot orter be done. I'll look up the cards for 'im and see wot 'is Signs is. I'd like to see 'im married and settled down.'

'Perhaps you mean to marry him yourself, Elizabeth?'

She gave a snort of indignation. 'Me! 'E's not my style. Give me a young man who can set off a bright necktie an' a white waistcoat with a nice watch an' albert 'ung on to it. But Mr. Roarings' now, 'e'd do well for some one who 'ad settled down, like, with quiet sort o' tastes. I got some one in my mind's eye for 'im already.'

From the moment that Elizabeth took his destiny in hand William was no longer safe, I felt sure. The Signs began to get to work upon him.

'William,' I said to him one day, 'Elizabeth means to marry you.'

'Why should I marry Elizabeth?' he asked placidly.

'I don't mean that she herself is to be the blushing bride. She prefers a man with a taste in waistcoats, a flowing auburn moustache, and a tendency to bright neckties, none of which qualities or quantities you possess. She means to get you married to some one else.'

William slowly removed his pipe from his mouth and regarded me with intense earnestness. He is not the sort of person who lets his emotions ripple to the surface, so his serious mien surprised me. He raised his hand in a prophetic attitude and began to speak. 'Dr. Johnson has rightly said that the incommodities of a single life are necessary and certain, but those of a conjugal state are avoidable. Excellent philosophy. Sooner than get married, my dear madame, I would walk in the wilderness, conversing with no man; I would fly to the fastnesses of Tibet; I would make of myself a hermit in a cave that was strongly barricaded. I would eschew tobacco. I would pay, to the uttermost farthing, any bachelor tax imposed by the State.'

'Do you so utterly abhor the idea of marriage?' I asked, profoundly astonished.

'I do,' said William.

A strange sound broke on our ears. It seemed to come through the keyhole, and resembled the contemptuous sniff with which Elizabeth always expresses incredulity. But, of course, it

Florence A. Kilpatrick

couldn't have been that.

As I have said, Elizabeth never listens at doors.

CHAPTER VII

(William - although he has a great regard for Pepys - does not himself keep a diary. From time to time, however, he 'chronicles the outstanding events in his career,' as he puts it. The following is one of William's 'chronicles,' which shows more knowledge than I have of the happenings in this chapter.)

William's Story: The more I think of it the more terrible the thing becomes from every aspect. Who could have thought that I, only a few days ago placidly drifting down the stream of life, should be jerked into such a maelstrom of difficulties? I must, however, try to think calmly. As Dr. Johnson has said, 'One of the principal themes of moral instruction is the art of bearing calamities.'

Let me try to narrate the events in their order - to trace, as far as possible, how this particular calamity occurred.

It began with Elizabeth. Or, I should say, she was the bearer of those disastrous tidings which have robbed me of my peace of mind and given me nights of sleepless horror.

Elizabeth, I ought to explain, is employed at the house of my friends, the Warringtons, as domestic worker. Up to the time of which I write I had barely observed the girl, beyond remarking that she was exceedingly lank as to form, and had a distressing habit of breathing very heavily when serving at table, due, I thought, to asthmatic tendencies.

Florence A. Kilpatrick

I learned later that it only betokened anxiety lest she should drop the various vessels she was handing round.

The circumstances which brought her particularly under my notice were singular. I had called at the Warringtons' one evening to have a smoke and chat with Henry, as is my wont. Elizabeth, after showing me into the study, told me that her master had gone out, but asked me to wait as he was expected to return every minute. I settled myself down, therefore, reached out for the tobacco jar, while my feet sought the familiar ledge below the mantelpiece, when I observed that Elizabeth was hovering in my vicinity.

'Excuse me, sir,' she said, speaking with apparent hesitation, 'but - but - do you mind if I speak to you?'

'Why shouldn't you speak to me if you want to?' I said, surprised and rather puzzled.

'Well, you see, sir, it's a bit 'ard to tell you. I dunno how to begin exactly - makes me feel like a cat treadin' on 'ot plates.' I quote exactly the rough vernacular of the lower classes in which she habitually expresses herself.

'There is no necessity for you to feel like a cat - or any other animal - treading on plates hot or otherwise when unburdening yourself to me,' I said kindly and benevolently, to put her at her ease. As a matter of fact, I half surmised the cause of her embarrassment. No doubt she had broken some object of value and wished me to act as intermediary with her mistress in the matter. I have frequently heard Mrs. Warrington complain of her ever-recurring breakages.

'If I can assist you in any way,' I continued, 'and intervene -'

'Inter-wot?' said Elizabeth.

'Er - perhaps you desire me to put in a good word for you with your mistress -'

'Do I *not*,' she broke in. 'I can put in all the good words *I* want meself - yes, an' a few more, too.'

I was pondering on the remarkable formation of this sentence which lent itself neither to analysis nor parsing, when her next words arrested my instant attention.

'It's about Miss Marryun I wanted to speak to you,' she said.

I stared. Why on earth should she speak to me about Miss Warrington, Henry's sister? I have not noticed her closely, but she is a quiet enough female, I believe, though possessed of an irritating habit of constantly pressing quite unnecessary ash-trays on a man.

To my surprise Elizabeth closed the door at this point and, coming up to me, whispered in a strange husky voice: 'That's just where all the trouble begins. It's what I overheerd 'er sayin' about you.'

I must confess to feeling rather startled. Then I remembered Mrs. Warrington had often commented on Elizabeth's curious proclivities for 'overhearing.' I looked at her coldly. I had not the slightest intention of becoming her confidant.

'Well, well, my good girl,' I retorted briskly, 'listeners never hear any good of themselves - or of other people either, I suppose. So, if you please, we will drop the subject.' I then picked up a book and held it before me to signify that the parley was at an end.

Elizabeth snorted. The term is vulgar, I know, but no other expression is adequate. 'Oo was listenin', I'd like to know?' she asked. 'I sed *overheerd*. The door was well on the jar and I was dustin' the 'all when I 'ears Miss Marryun a-moanin' and a-sobbin' like. Missus was talkin' to 'er and soothin' 'er. "Don't carry on so," she ses, "for I tells you, it's no use."

'"No use," ses Miss Marryun in a choked sort o' voice, "why is it no use? I love 'im, I adore 'im. Oh, Willyum, Willyum, you'll break my 'art if you go on with this yeer cold indifference -"'

'Stop,' I interposed sternly. At any other time I might have smiled at the girl's quaint phraseology. But I did not smile just then. *Dulce est desipere in loco.* Wild as the story sounded, it was making me feel decidedly uncomfortable. A slight perspiration had broken out on my forehead. But I threw a strong note of assurance into my voice as I went on: 'Girl, this is a monstrous action on your part to listen - er - overhear at doors and repeat conversations of a most delicate nature to a third party.'

'What-ho,' put in Elizabeth.

'Now let me show you the mistake under which you are labouring. It is true my name is William, but William is a common name. I have remarked, indeed, that the world is pretty full of Williams. Miss Warrington was in no way referring to me.'

'I don't think,' commented Elizabeth.

'Evidently you don't,' I said severely, 'or you would not make such absurd statements.'

'I ain't done yet,' went on this diabolical creature. 'You say it wasn't meant fer you? Listen. When Miss Marryun goes on wringin' 'er 'ands an' sobbin', "I love my Willyum," missus ses, "But 'ow can you love such a big ugly brute of a man wot's allus throwin' 'is tobacco ash about the place, and scrapin' the fendy with 'is feet and never wears a fancy westcoat even at evernin' parties. 'Ow can you love him?" she arsks.

'"I don't know myself," ses Miss Marryun, "but there it is. I'd rather die than live without my Willyum."'

'Silence,' I burst out fiercely, 'do you think I don't know that all this is pure invention on your part - for what reason I, as yet, cannot tell. How dare you concoct such tales?'

'Wait till I've finished, please, sir. The missus, she ses, "But Marryun, my pore dear, it's no use lovin' 'im. 'E ses to me 'is very self the other day, 'e ses, 'Sooner than get married I'd go and dwell in the wilderness, I'd go to Tibbet, be an 'ermit in a cave, give up baccy, and give away every farthin' I 'ad in the world.'"'

A feeling of acute horror swept over me. With a crash my favourite pipe fell from my nerveless fingers and was smashed to atoms on the fender. There was truth in the girl's fantastic story after all. I recalled using such expressions as those when, a little time before, I was discussing conjugal difficulties in a talk with Mrs. Warrington. Obviously the girl could not have made the thing up. I passed my hand wildly across my brow. 'But what have I done that she should fall in love with me? What is there about me to attract any woman?'

'Nothink, as I can see,' she retorted, 'but with a woman's heart there's no knowin' an' there's no tellin'. P'raps you've managed to throw dust in her eyes.'

'I have thrown nothing - I mean, Miss Warrington and I are only slightly acquainted with each other. I have, indeed, barely noticed her. And now you tell me this horrible thing.'

She bridled. 'Wot's 'orrible about it? You ought to be glad. Most men would be proud to marry a young lady 'oo's got such a light 'and for pastry, and can mend up an old pair o' pants to make 'em look like new. She's just the sort of wife -'

'"Wife,"' I interrupted, '"marry"? What do you mean by those words, girl? Do you think for one instant if all the females in Christendom were to fall in love with me I would *marry* any one of them! No, a thousand times, no. I repeat I will never, *never* marry.'

Florence A. Kilpatrick

'I 'eard yer,' said Elizabeth, 'and do you sit there and mean to tell me that you're going to break a gentle woman's 'eart deliberate?'

The imputation caused me to shudder from head to foot. 'No, no, Elizabeth. If I have unwittingly caused the lady pain I am deeply remorseful. But she must, as soon as possible, be disillusioned.'

'Dish-who?' said Elizabeth. In this peculiar and baffling way does she express herself. It makes a sustained conversation extremely difficult and, at times, almost impossible.

'She must be brought to dislike me, I mean. In this matter I must ask you to help me.' I took a ten-shilling note from my pocket. 'If, from time to time, you will talk to Miss Warrington of my many faults - you can invent what you like -'

'Shan't need to invent much in the way o' faults,' put in the monstrous girl. 'But it's my belief she likes you for 'em. Some women are made like that. Anyway,' she handed me back the note which I had endeavoured to press into her warm, moist palm. 'I'm not wantin' this. I'm not goin' to take blood money to 'elp to break any woman's 'eart.'

It sounded really terrible viewed in that light. 'There is no need for you to put it in that coarse way,' I said, my temper rising. 'I only ask you to help me to regain my peace of mind and secure Miss Warrington's happiness.'

'Well, if you put it like that o' course,' she said, her fingers closing over the note, 'I'm not the one to refuse good money. I'm willin' to do all I can to make you an' Miss Marryun happy.' With a broad grin she sidled out of the room.

As for me, I gathered up the fragments of my pipe and departed. I no longer wished to talk to Henry just then. I wanted to be alone to think, to consider my strategic position.

I must go away to some remote place, perhaps not Tibet, but at any rate a quiet spot in the country fully twenty miles out of London. Before going, however, I must in some way show Miss Warrington the utter folly of her illusions regarding my unfortunate self. Nothing must be left undone to achieve that object.

Alas, what troubles, what unending anxiety a woman can cause a man! After getting over this difficulty, I swear I will not even converse with any one of them again. In the meantime I must invoke the aid of this wretched girl Elizabeth. *Necessitas non habet legem.* Elizabeth is that most irritating necessity.

CHAPTER VIII

Elizabeth often speaks of the time when she poisoned The Kid. She says she never had such a 'turn' in all her life, and wouldn't go through such an experience again for all the money in the world. Neither, indeed, would I, or Henry, or Marion. Looking back on the matter, I don't think The Kid cared for it either.

It was a peaceful summer evening. The Kid had just gone to bed and we - Henry, Marion and I - had foregathered in the study. Marion spends most of her time with us, being one of those delightfully restful persons who doesn't need to be 'entertained,' who doesn't talk to you if you want to do a little writing at meal times, and is altogether a desirable visitor. Thus, at the moment of which I write, we sat in perfect amity and silence, Henry working, I working, while every time I looked up my eyes fell on the gratifying vision of dear Marion making a blouse for me. Suddenly the door opened and Elizabeth entered.

'That there medicine you told me to give Miss Moira,' she said. 'I just been looking at it and I see it's got your name on the bottle.' She held it out to me as she spoke.

'Why is The Kid taking medicine?' inquired Marion.

'It's only a little tonic the doctor prescribed. But,' I stared at the bottle Elizabeth had brought in, 'this is my medicine. The chemist must have mixed up the prescriptions when I took them to him.' Suddenly I sprang to my feet. 'Great Heavens! My tonic contains strychnine!'

'And as you've been taking it for some time, I expect the dose has been increased,' said Marion excitedly. 'How much did you give her, Elizabeth?'

'A teaspoonful, miss, as usual.'

I wrung my hands. 'I take only six drops at a time myself! What are we to do?'

'One place I was at,' put in Elizabeth, 'the master was rather fond of a drop too much, an' 'e come 'ome very late one night an' drank spirits o' salt thinkin' it was something else, so we give 'im stuff to bring it up agen.'

'Of course,' said Marion, 'that's the very thing.' Long ago, during the war, she worked in a hospital, so she affects to know something of medicines. 'Give The Kid an emetic at once. Ipecac. Dose 5 minims. Repeat, if necessary. Or salt and water. I'll dash off to the doctor's and ask him what's to be done.' And seizing the bottle she hurried out.

The Kid was sitting up in bed eating her supper when Elizabeth, Henry and I burst breathlessly into her room. Her face was shining with quiet contentment.

'Look, Mama, dear,' she said, 'at the beautiful baked custard Elizabeth has made for my supper. Wasn't it kind of her?'

I snatched the custard away from her grasp. 'Don't eat another mouthful,' I panted, 'you're going to have an emetic. You must be sick at once.'

Mutely questioning inexorable Fate, she raised large, contemplative eyes to mine. '*Must* I, Mama? Can't I finish my custard first?'

There is about The Kid's character a stoic philosophy, blended, since she has known Elizabeth, with a certain fatalism. Her habit of saying '*Must* I?' when faced with a disagreeable duty, indicates her outlook on life. If those in authority declare she must, then there is no more to be said about it. They represent Fate in action. She now yielded up the custard with a sigh, but obediently drank the mixture I handed her. There was a pause.

'How are you feeling, dear?' I inquired.

'Quite well, thank you, Mama, dear. May I have my custard now?'

'You ought not to be feeling well,' I said, puzzled. 'You'd better have some more drops.'

'Oh, must I, Mama?'

'Yes, dear. Drink this.' I now gave her a slightly larger dose. There was a still longer pause, and Henry, Elizabeth and I waited for her to speak, or express emotion of some sort. At last she opened her lips and said, 'May I have -'

'A basin?' inquired Elizabeth, darting forward.

'- my custard, now, if you please, Elizabeth?'

'No,' I said sternly. 'It's very strange that the ipecac, has had no effect.'

'Try salt and water. There's more about it, like,' remarked Elizabeth. 'I'll fetch some.'

'And hurry,' Henry commanded, 'every moment's delay is making the thing more serious.'

'Now drink this salt and water, darling,' I urged The Kid when Elizabeth reappeared.

'Oh, *must* I, Mama?'

'Yes. Your life depends upon it.'

She drank rather hastily at that. There was a long, long pause while Elizabeth, Henry and I gazed into each other's eyes and - waited.

'How do you feel now?' I asked at last with strained anxiety.

'I'm feeling rather sick now, thank you, Mama, dear. But perhaps I could manage a little of my cus -'

'No,' I interrupted. 'Can't you be sick, child?'

'I'm afraid I can't, Mama.'

'Then why can't you?' Henry burst out. 'It's dreadful - most unnatural.'

'She's got a stummick like an 'orse,' commented Elizabeth.

'Prompt action is vital,' put in Henry firmly. 'There are other emetics. Mustard and -'

'I've always 'eard that soap and water's good for turnin' any one over,' began Elizabeth.

'Soap and water!' I echoed, 'yes, that sounds the worst - the best, I mean. Get it at once, Elizabeth.'

'Enough to make a good lather, should you think, 'm?'

'Oh, *must* I?' wailed the Kid, still questioning inexorable Fate.

We all united in preparing the soap and water to avoid delay. Elizabeth boiled the water. Henry cut the soap into small flakes, and I beat it up into a lather. Then, now in a condition of feverish anxiety, I handed The Kid the foaming mixture.

'Drink,' I panted.

'Oh, mus -' she began.

'Don't say that again!' I exclaimed, overwrought by the intensity of my emotions. 'Can't you see how serious it is, child? You might die any minute.'

She drank off the contents of the glass without further question.

'Well, that ought to do it,' commented Henry, looking at a few iridescent bubbles at the bottom of the glass. 'I made it strong.'

There was a strained silence when I almost seemed to hear my own heart beats. 'How - how - do you feel, now, darling?' I asked at last.

'Dreadful, thank you, Mama, dear.'

'That isn't enough,' I cried in anguish. 'Can't you -?'

'No, I can't, Mama.'

'This is terrible,' I broke out, fast becoming hysterical. 'What is to be done! Can nothing save her?'

'I suppose the doctor will bring along a stomach pump,' said Henry, trying to soothe me.

'Oh, must he?' moaned The Kid (ignored).

'Get 'er to put 'er finger down 'er throat,' suggested Elizabeth brightly; 'that'll work it.'

It was the last straw. The Kid, though still dutiful, was utterly outraged. 'No, no, I won't,' she cried in open rebellion.

She looked unhappy. The soap and water had evidently met the allied forces of ipecac. and salt, and a fierce battle was, no doubt, in progress in her interior at the moment. 'I won't,' she repeated desperately.

'Do try, darling,' implored Henry, 'and I'll give you a whole shilling.'

'No, no, *no*. I don't want any shillings.' Judging by her expression the soap must have commenced an encircling movement, and the salt and ipecac. were hurrying up reserves. 'I won't put my finger down my throat.'

'What are we to do?' I said, wringing my hands. 'I never knew her to be so obstinate. Why, oh, why doesn't the doctor come? The child is beginning to look so strange already.'

'Well, wot I'd do if I was you,' suggested Elizabeth, 'is to begin the doses all over again -'

'Good,' said Henry. 'Firstly the ipecac. -'

'Oh, must I?' interrupted The Kid.

To my intense relief Marion dashed in at that moment. 'Have you given her an emetic?' she demanded breathlessly.

Elizabeth, Henry and I gathered round her with the necessary information.

'She has had several. Ipecac. -'

'Twice.'

'Salt and water -'

'A cupful.'

'Warm soap and water -'

'One glass.'

'And,' I concluded, now in tears, 'she won't be sick - simply *won't!*'

'I do want to, *auntie*,' explained The Kid, her child's sense of justice receiving mortal blows, 'but I can't *be -*'

Marion stood and gazed at her in awe. 'It's wonderful,' she murmured, 'amazing! I think, perhaps, *The Lancet* would be interested in a letter on the subject.'

'But what did the doctor say?' broke in Henry. 'Is he coming?'

'No,' said Marion, 'he -'

'Why not?' I asked feverishly.

'Because he said it was all right directly he tasted the contents of the bottle. But to make quite sure he 'phoned to your chemist, who, it appears, put your name on the bottle instead of The Kid's. He was awfully sorry and apologetic.'

'Sorry!' I echoed, 'apologetic! Why, the man's a monster. To think of all I've suffered through his carelessness.' I sank down on a chair. 'I'm quite overwrought.'

'There's no harm done, thank goodness,' said Marion.

'"All's well that ends well,"' quoted Henry.

'I'm fair relieved to get that load orf my mind,' supplemented Elizabeth.

'Mama, dear,' put in The Kid, glad, no doubt, that at last she was able to please, 'I think that now I really can *be -*'

'It doesn't matter now, darling,' I explained. 'You'd better lie perfectly still and let it pass off.'

'Must I, Mama?'

We all moved towards the door. The relief from the strain was apparent in our joyous faces and lightened mien. We sang out 'Good-night' to The Kid, and went out laughing and chatting. Half-way down the stairs we heard her calling.

'Mama, dear.'

'What is it?' we all asked in chorus.

'Please may I have my custard *now*?'

Florence A. Kilpatrick

CHAPTER IX

*Being an extract from the diary of Miss Marion Warrington:
Thursday.* A most remarkable and perplexing thing has
happened. Never, for a moment, could I have dreamed of such
an improbable and embarrassing occurrence.

It was Elizabeth who first brought it to my notice, and I can
only wish she had never made that strange discovery which is
causing me so much uneasiness. I was spending the day with
Netta, and had gone into the kitchen for a moment, when
Elizabeth asked if she might speak to me in confidence. This
rather surprised me, because she does not, as a rule, show such
diffidence about speaking (in confidence or otherwise) to any
one.

'Is it anything very important?' I inquired.

She seemed to hesitate and then jerked out, 'Well, miss, it's
about that there Mr. Roarings.'

I at once felt rather troubled on Netta's account. Perhaps
Elizabeth was on the verge of giving notice as a protest against
the extra work involved by having that monstrously untidy
man about the place. Why Netta tolerates him with his
slovenly habits is beyond my comprehension.

'What has he been doing now?' I asked. 'Surely he hasn't
started another invention?' I never before realized what a
thoroughly untidy, disordered business inventing could be

until I saw him at it.

'Oh, no, miss, nothin' like that, only - only - well, it was what I see when 'e was standin' in the droring-room the other day, an' I was just at the door -'

'I quite understand, Elizabeth. He has burnt a hole in that beautiful pile carpet.'

'No, miss, he -'

'Then he has scorched the rose silk tapestry on the couch!' It is my opinion that he should not be allowed in the drawing-room at all. He isn't safe with a pipe in his mouth or a box of matches in his pocket. Henry ought to take out a special insurance against Mr. Rawlings.

'No, it's nothin' like that, miss. As I was sayin', 'e was standin' in the droring-room. The door was wide open. I was just goin' in to dust an' then I sees that 'e's 'oldin' your photo in 'is 'ands, that big one in the silver frame. 'E was starin' at it wild-like, and a-mutterin' to 'isself. I 'eard 'im say, quite distinct, "Oh, Marryun, Marryun, my beautiful darlin', 'ow I adore you," ses e. "I'm not 'arf mad about you." An' then 'e starts kissin' the photo until I thinks 'e'll crack the glarss of the frame with 'is passion and 'ot breath.'

I stared at her, scarcely able to believe the evidence of my own ears. Then, remembering that she is a girl greatly given to a maudlin kind of sentiment, I was reassured. 'You have been mistaken,' I said with quiet dignity. 'Mr. Rawlings is incapable of such a display as you have just described. If, as you say, he was holding my photo in his hand, it was, no doubt, for the purpose of using it as an ash-tray.'

'Never seen 'im use an ash-tray,' commented Elizabeth.

'Being in the drawing-room he might, for once, have had some qualms about the carpet,' I explained. Under his rugged

Florence A. Kilpatrick

exterior he may have a conscience. I rather doubt it myself, but one should never judge too harshly.

'Arter 'earing 'im say that,' went on Elizabeth, 'I didn't like to let 'im see I'd been in the room all the time, an' I was just goin' to creep out quiet when 'e starts talkin' to the photo again. "Marryun," 'e ses, "if I carn't 'ave you I'll go away in the wilderness, or be an 'ermit in a cave, or go an' live in Tibbet, or give away every farthin' I've got in the world." That's wot 'e sed, an' 'e looked so wild I was fair scared, miss.'

I stared at Elizabeth, quite unable to speak a word. The whole thing sounded so wildly improbable and yet she was obviously speaking the truth. She is, I should say, a girl of no imagination and, being entirely artless, could not possibly have invented such a thing. At last I found my voice, which sounded rather hollow. 'What a terrible thing,' I said.

'Why terrible?' she inquired.

Poor, simple girl, with her primitive views of life, how little she understood the delicate situation that had been created, or the significance of the words she had just repeated to me.

'I detest the idea of inflicting pain even on an animal,' I replied, 'and if, as you say, Mr. Rawlings appeared to be suffering on my account -'

''E was - agonies,' she put in.

'Well, is not the whole position dreadful? Mr. Rawlings is the last, the very last man, Elizabeth, in the whole world that I should think of in the way you mention.'

I could not repress a sigh as I spoke. How peculiar is the irony of fate. Why should I deny (particularly in this, my diary, which contains the outpourings of my soul) that I have often wished to win the love of some good strong man who could protect me in the battle of life and be willing, as it were, like the knights of old, to enter the lists for my sake. This I could in no way imagine Mr. Rawlings doing. My conception of the hero of my dreams may have varied from time to time, but never has it included even the smallest of the characteristics of William Rawlings. He reminds me of nothing so much as the very shaggiest bear I have ever seen at the Zoo - not even a nice white Polar bear, but one of those nondescript, snuff-coloured kinds that are all ragged ends from top to toe. That a man with such a rough exterior could be capable of such sickening sentimentality as Elizabeth had just described quite nauseated me. It made me dislike him more, if possible, than I had done before.

'Remember, Elizabeth,' I said, looking at her steadily, 'you must not repeat a word of this to any one. Mr. Rawlings must never know that he has been discovered in this -'

'Well, 'e knows that *I* know,' she interrupted.

I stared. 'What do you mean?'

'You see, me bein' in the room when 'e was a-kissin' of your fotograft, 'e looks up an' sees me afore I could get away, quiet, like. "Good lor', Elizabeth," 'e breaks out, "you don't mean to tell me that you sor everything, that you 'eard my 'eart strings burstin' in a manner of speakin'."

'"I'm afraid I did, sir," ses I, "I was just comin' in to dust an' your sighs bein' rather loud, I couldn't 'elp overhearing."

'"Listen," 'e ses, goin' ashy pale, "you must never tell 'er. I will win 'er in my own way," 'e ses. "In the meantime, 'ere is ten shillings, my good girl. Will you put in a word for me with Miss Worryington from time to time? She may not like me just yet, but I'll make 'er mine or blow my brains out."

'"I shouldn't do that, sir, if I was you," I ses, "leastways not yet until you see 'ow things turns out, like."

Florence A. Kilpatrick

'"I'm goin' to lead a better life," 'e goes on, "an' stop puttin' baccy ash in my pocket, an' dustin' my boots with my handkercher, an' all those little things that a gentle woman might find careless."'

'Elizabeth,' I put in weakly, 'this is terrible. I do not want Mr. Rawlings to make any sacrifices for me. I do not want Mr. Rawlings. Nothing in the world would make me consider his suit.'

'"Is suit's all right if it were well brushed an' pressed,' she said. 'An if 'e isn't quite a fancy style 'isself we can't all pick an' choose in this world. Don't go despisin' of 'im too much, miss. If 'e was properly done up, now, and sort o' dusted an' polished, like, 'e mightn't be so bad.'

I turned on her with burning indignation. 'How dare you openly assist his plans after confessing to taking his money as a bribe? Don't mention his name to me again, or I shall refuse to listen to you.'

She actually had the impertinence to look indignant. 'It's shame I cry on you, miss, for tryin' to break the pore man's 'eart. Then I s'pose I can't give 'im that there fotograft of you?'

'My photograph! Of all the unspeakable -'

'It was with 'im sayin' that if 'e only 'ad it to look at it might 'elp to parss all the dark 'ours 'e 'as to spend away from you. 'E sed 'e wanted it to look at wen 'e was lyin' awake at night, thinkin' of you.'

I strove to be reasonable. 'To let him have my photo, Elizabeth, would only encourage his mad ideas. No, all this must be stopped immediately. I shall take prompt measures. Once more, let me beg of you never to mention this painful occurrence to any one.' I turned to go out of the kitchen, but when I reached the door Elizabeth called to me. 'I wanted to ask you a favour, miss, if it isn't troublin' you too much,' she began.

'What is it?' I inquired rather absently, for my mind was very much disturbed just then.

'You see, miss, it's this way. I gotta young man wot's very poetick, like. 'E's always sendin' me portry copied from mottoes out o' crackers. It's very 'ard to keep up with 'im.'

'Then how do you want me to help you?' I asked, puzzled.

'I wondered if you'd be so kind as to copy me a bit o' portry I sor in one o' master's books. It sounds real pretty, but I can't get it down right. My 'andwritin' is that bad.' She took a leather-bound volume of Byron from the kitchen drawer. 'It's just this yere bit: -

"Yet, oh, yet thyself deceeve not,
Luv' may sink by slow decay;
But by suddint wrench beleeve not
'Earts can thus be torn away."'

'Have you had a quarrel with your young man?' I asked, perplexed at the strange selection of verse.

'No, miss, but 'e's 'overin' just now - you know what I mean. I want to bring 'im up to the scratch, like.'

I could not help thinking what blunt direct methods the lower classes employ in affairs of the heart. In our walk in life the sending of such lines to a gentleman who had not declared himself would be considered almost indelicate. However, I wrote out the absurd lines for the girl without comment, and rescued Henry's volume of Byron, which I felt would not improve in appearance by contact wit h the meatchopper, knife-board and other miscellaneous objects which she keeps in the kitchen drawer. It is a pity Netta does not exercise stricter supervision over Elizabeth. The girl seems to do what she likes.

Florence A. Kilpatrick

'You had better ask permission from Mrs. Warrington before taking books into the kitchen,' I said with gentle reproof. 'They might get lost or soiled.'

'Right-o!' said Elizabeth. 'An' do you reely mean that you're not a-goin' to give your fotograft to Mr. Roarings?'

'Indeed not,' I said vehemently, 'don't dare to suggest the idea to me again. If Mr. Rawlings ever speaks of it to you, you can tell him how amazed and indignant I was.'

'Right-o!' said Elizabeth, as I hurried out of the kitchen.

On thinking the whole matter over I must admit I am greatly perturbed. I am not like those women who glory in winning a man's love for the mere gratification of their vanity. I know myself how much one can suffer from unrequited affection, and I am steadily determined to cure Mr. Rawlings of his love-madness by every means in my power.

CHAPTER X

The study door burst open and one end of Elizabeth - the articulate end - was jerked into view.

'Wot will you 'ave for lunch, 'm?' she demanded breathlessly. 'Lamb or 'am?'

Abruptly recalled from the realms of fiction writing I looked up a little dazed. 'Lamb or 'am,' I repeated dully, 'lamorram? Er - ram, I think, please, Elizabeth.'

Having thus disposed of my domestic obligations for the day, I returned to my writing. I was annoyed therefore to see the other end of Elizabeth travel round the doorway and sidle into the room. Her pretext for entering - that of dusting the roll-top desk with her apron - was a little thin, for she has not the slightest objection to dust. I rather think it cheers her up to see it about the place. Obviously she had come in to make conversation. I laid down my pen with a sigh.

'I yeerd from my young man this morning,' she began. A chill foreboding swept over me. (I will explain why in a minute.)

'Do you mean the boiler one?' I asked.

''Im wot belongs to the Amalgamated Serciety of Boiler-makers,' she corrected with dignity. 'Well, they've moved 'is 'eadquarters from London to Manchester.'

Florence A. Kilpatrick

There was a tense silence, broken only by Elizabeth's hard breathing on a brass paper-weight ere she polished it with her sleeve.

'If 'e goes to Manchester, there I goes,' she went on; 'I suppose I'd quite easy get a situation there?'

'Quite easy,' I acquiesced in a hollow voice.

She went out leaving me chill and dejected. Not that I thought for a moment that I was in imminent danger of losing her. I knew full well that this was but a ruse on the part of the young man to disembarrass himself of Elizabeth, and, if he had involved the entire Amalgamated Society of Boilermakers in the plot, that only proved how desperate he was.

I have very earnest reasons for wishing that Elizabeth could have a 'settled' young man. You see, as I have previously explained, she never retains the same one for many weeks at a time. It isn't her fault, poor girl. She would be as true as steel if she had a chance; she would cling to any one of them through thick and thin, following him to the ends of the earth if necessary.

It is they who are fickle, and the excuses they make to break away from her are both varied and ingenious. During the War, of course, they always had the pretext of being ordered to the Front at a moment's notice, and were not, it appears, allowed to write home on account of the Censor. Elizabeth used to blame Lloyd George for these defects of organization. Even to this day she is extremely bitter against the Government.

In fact, she is bitter against every one when her love affairs are not running smoothly. The entire household suffers in consequence. She is sullen and obstinate; she is always on the verge of giving notice. And the way she breaks things in her abstraction is awful. Elizabeth's illusions and my crockery always get shattered together. My rose-bowl of Venetian glass got broken when the butcher threw her over for the housemaid next door. Half a dozen tumblers, a basin and several odd plates came in two in her hands after the grocer's assistant went away suddenly to join the silent Navy. And nearly the whole of a dinner service was sacrificed when Lloyd George peremptorily ordered her young man in the New Army to go to Mesopotamia and stay there for at least three years without leave.

Those brief periods when Elizabeth's young men are in the incipient stages of paying her marked attention are agreeable to everybody. Elizabeth, feeling no doubt in her rough untutored way that God's in his Heaven and all's right with the world, sings at her work; she shows extraordinary activity when going about her duties. She does unusual things like remembering to polish the brasses every week - indeed, you have only to step in the hall and glance at the stair rods to discover the exact stage of her latest 'affair.' I remember once when one ardent swain (who she declared was 'in the flying corpse') got to the length of offering her marriage before he flew away, she cleaned the entire house down in her enthusiasm - and had actually got to the cellars before he vanished out of her life.

You will now understand why I was dejected at the perfidy of the follower belonging to the Boilermakers' Society. I saw a dreary period of discomfort ahead of me. Worst of all I was expecting the Boscombes to dinner that very week. They had not before visited us, and Henry was anxious to impress Mr. Boscombe, he being a publisher. It is surprising, when you come to think of it, how full the world is of writers trying to make a good impression on publishers. Yet no one has met the publisher who ever tries to make a good impression on any one.

I will not elaborate the situation as it stood. All I can say is that there is no earthly possibility of making a good impression on any living thing if Elizabeth is in one of her bad moods. And it would be no use explaining the case to Mrs. Boscombe, because she has no sense of humour; or to Mr. Boscombe, because he likes a good dinner.

Florence A. Kilpatrick

Finally, the Domestic Bureau failed me. Hitherto they had always been able to supply me with a temporary waitress on the occasion of dinner parties. Now it appeared these commodities had become pearls of great price which could no longer be cast before me and mine (at the modest fee of ten shillings a night) without at least fourteen days' notice.

The Bureau promised to do its best for me, of course, but reminded me that women were scarce. I asked, with bitterness, what had become of the surplus million we heard so much about. They replied with politeness that, judging from the number of applications received, they must be the million in search of domestics.

Returning home from the Bureau, I found Elizabeth studying a time-table.

'I see it's a 'undred and eighty-three miles to Manchester,' she commented, 'an' the fare's 15s. 5 1/2d.'

'That's an old time-table you've got,' I hastened to remark, 'it is now L2 13s. 7 1/2d. - return fare.'

'I shan't want no return ticket,' said Elizabeth grimly.

Sickening outlook, wasn't it?

$$* \quad * \quad * \quad * \quad *$$

The day of my dinner-party dawned fair and bright, but Elizabeth was raging. Things got so bad, in fact, that about mid-day I decided I must telephone to the Boscombes and tell them Henry had suddenly been taken ill; and I was just looking up the doctor's book to find something especially virulent and infectious for Henry, when Elizabeth came in. Amazing to relate, her face was wreathed in smiles.

'They've sent from the Domestic Boorow,' she began.

'What!' I exclaimed, 'did they get me a waitress after all?'

She smirked. 'They've sent a man this time. A footman 'e was before the War, but 'e didn't take it up again arter 'e was demobbed. Just now, bein' out of a job 'e's takin' tempory work and -'

'He seems to have told you quite a lot about himself already,' I interposed.

She smirked again. 'I 'adn't been talkin' to 'im ten minutes afore 'e arsked me wot was my night out. 'E isn't arf a one.'

'It seems he isn't,' I agreed. And I sent up a silent prayer of thankfulness to Heaven and the Domestic Bureau. 'But what about the Amalgamated boilermaker?'

'Oh, 'im!' She tossed her head. "E can go to - Manchester.'

CHAPTER XI

'Have you observed William closely, recently, Netta?' Henry asked me. 'Something seems to have happened to him?'

'Why should I observe William?' I demanded, puzzled, 'he is not the sort of man a woman would observe, closely or otherwise.'

'That is exactly one of the reasons why I like him - you leave him alone,' remarked that horrid Henry. 'I can talk to him without your distracting his attention by flirting with him.'

I felt wounded. 'Henry, this is monstrous.'

'You cannot deny, my dear, that I have brought men - fluent conversationalists - round here for a pleasant evening's debate only to see them become abstracted and monosyllabic directly you appear.'

'You can't blame me for that, Henry.'

'Yes, I do. You deliberately seek to interest them. I've seen you at it. You spare no pains or powder to gain your object. Don't dare to deny it.'

Chastened, I replied meekly: 'Dear Henry, I love my fellow-creatures - if they haven't beards,' I added hastily. 'After all, doesn't the Scripture command it?'

'But you don't love William.'

'The Scripture says nothing at all about William,' I replied decidedly. 'I - er - tolerate him. What is this you tell me about something having happened to him?'

'He's growing peculiar.'

'*More* peculiar, I suppose you mean?'

'His manner is erratic and changed. It isn't another invention, because when he is inventing he is merely monosyllabic, with spasms of muttering and an increased tendency to knock things over. Now he's altogether different. It's the trend of his conversation that puzzles me. He talks of love.'

'Love and William,' I remarked, 'are as incompatible as acids and alkalis. In what way does he touch on the subject? With bitterness or curiosity?

'Both, I should say. For one thing he is most 'anxious to know what are the effects of unrequited affection, and if the results can be serious. Seems strange, doesn't it?'

'It's passing strange, Henry.'

'You don't think he's fallen in love with you, Netta?'

'What makes you suggest he's fallen in love with me?'

'Because he comes in contact with no other woman beyond you and his landlady, who, I understand, is over sixty and weighs fifteen stone - so it must be you if it's anybody.' (This is a Scotsman's way of paying a compliment; if you can follow the workings of his mind up to the source of the idea you will see he means well.)

'That William should fall in love seems incredible - and entirely unnecessary,' I commented. 'There must be some other explanation of his manner. As he's coming to dinner to-night, I'll watch and see if I can find anything unusually strange about him.'

When William made his appearance, therefore, I observed him intently. Surely enough I was struck by the fact that he was changed in some subtle way. He looked dejected. Of course it was impossible to see much of his expression, owing to his face being almost entirely obliterated with hair, but what was visible was extremely sad.

Then a strange thing happened. As soon as we were alone he began to exhibit signs of acute mental distress, and to my astonishment burst out, 'Mrs. Warrington, there is something I wanted to - er - ask you. You are a woman for whom I have a profound respect; though you are inclined by character to be *un peu moqueuse*, you have, I feel, an exceedingly tender heart.'

I felt uneasy. 'Yes, William, it is tender - but not for everybody,' I added warningly. Really, it was going to be very awkward if he, in his elephantine way, had conceived an infatuation for me. My conscience was perfectly clear - I had not encouraged him in any way, but nevertheless I did not wish to see him suffer from unrequited affection. It would be so awkward in many ways. William, even in his sane moods, has a dreadful habit of knocking things over. If the abstraction of the lover descended upon him, it was going to have a dire effect on our household goods.

'Because your heart is tender,' he pursued, 'you will be able to realize the difficulty of my - er - you can better understand the sufferings of others. Do you think an ill-placed affection can be combated - that is, in time, be utterly stamped out?'

'I do, William,' I said firmly, 'but it must be stamped effectively, you understand. No half measures, you know.'

'Yes, yes, I quite see that,' he said eagerly. 'Then do you think in such a case it would help matters if a man - if one of the parties, I mean - went right away. You know the adage, "Out of sight out of mind"?'

I pondered. It would, I knew, be a great denial to William if he was debarred from coming about our place - almost the only home he had ever known. Henry, too, would be lost with no one to argue with. If you want to manage a Scotsman properly see that he gets plenty of argument, and he'll rarely develop any other vice. No, the pair must not be separated.

'There is another adage, William, which says, "Absence makes the heart grow fonder,"' I said, 'so I think, after all, you - I mean he, had better stay.'

William looked relieved. 'You think that I - er - I mean one - ought to face it?'

'I am sure one should,' I acquiesced.

William pressed my hand gratefully, and I sighed as I examined his physiognomy in the hope of finding one attractive feature. I sighed again as I finished my inspection. What a pity, I thought, that he had not just a little dash about him, even the merest *soupcon* of fascination, in order to make the situation interesting. He was still holding my hand as the door opened and Elizabeth shot into view with the declaration, 'Dinner's in.'

We have a massive and imposing looking gong erected in the hall for the sole purpose of announcing when meals are ready, but nothing will induce Elizabeth to make use of it. If we are upstairs she hails us from below with such expressions as 'Come on, now, it's getting cold,' or, 'I won't bring it in till you're all 'ere, so mind you 'urry.'

If William had appeared strange, it struck me that Marion - who was also dining with us that evening - was even stranger. For one thing, I regret to say, she was exceedingly rude to William. She does not like him, I know, but he was after all

Florence A. Kilpatrick

our guest, and she was not justified in remarking, when he upset his wine on the tablecloth, and knocked over an adjacent salt-cellar, 'If there's anything in the world I loathe, it is a clumsy man.'

'I must admit I *am* extremely clumsy - like an elephant, in fact,' came the soft answer from William.

It did not turn away Marion's wrath. 'So I see,' she snapped.

I kicked her gently under the table. 'Marion, *dear*,' I remonstrated.

'Nothing in the world will ever improve me,' continued William.

'I'm sure of it,' replied Marion, 'it's in your system.'

She seemed in a most contrary mood that evening. For instance, William had remarked quite nicely and affably that he considered smoking pernicious for women. He said his mother had always declared it was, and he thought they were better without it. Whereupon Marion, who dislikes the weed as a general rule, immediately got up, took a cigarette from the box on the table and asked William for a light.

'I suppose I'm shocking you terribly,' she remarked to him.

'I don't think there's anything you could do that would shock me now,' he replied. It was rather a peculiar retort, especially as he laid a faint accent on the 'you.' Evidently he wished to have his revenge for what she had said to him at dinner.

'I smoke even in bed,' said Marion, regarding him steadily. I was at a loss to understand why she told this deliberate falsehood.

'So do I,' said William calmly.

'I smoke in the bath,' continued Marion.

'By Jove, so do I,' said William, looking at her with a new interest. 'But don't you find it rather awkward when you're washing your back?'

Marion looked rather scandalized, as though she considered William's remark in bad taste. But she had only herself to blame after all. She was silent and rather moody after that, until the episode of the photograph occurred. We were assembled in the drawing-room, and I suddenly noticed that a photo of Marion which stands on the mantelpiece had been removed from its frame.

'Why, Marion, what has become of your photo?' I inquired.

There was, after all, nothing unusual in its disappearance. It was one that she did not like and she had often threatened to remove it. What was my astonishment now to see her spring to her feet and, going white with suppressed anger, exclaim, 'Who has dared to take it? It is a piece of unwarrantable impertinence. Who has *dared*, I say?'

I saw William looking at her in surprise - it was, indeed, something even deeper than that. Fascinated horror seems a more apt expression.

'I insist on its being recovered,' went on Marion.

A strange exclamation from William made us all look at him. 'Women,' he said, 'are beyond me - utterly beyond me, I repeat.'

'I'm glad you admit it,' snapped Marion.

'In guile,' he continued coldly. 'I suppose, now, you have never heard of a woman thrusting her photograph where it is not wanted accompanied by verse of an amorous character?'

Marion looked contemptuously at him. 'What on earth are you raving about?' she inquired.

Henry and I intervened at this moment and changed the subject, feeling that a quarrel between them was imminent. It was all very strange and puzzling. But the strangest thing was yet to come. I had accompanied Marion upstairs to put on her cloak before departure, and when we descended William had vanished. Henry related that he was just answering a call on the 'phone when he saw William dash past him into the small lobby off the hall, possess himself of hat and coat, and, after muttering some words of apology, go forth into the darkness.

'How eccentric - and ill-behaved, too,' I commented. 'It looks almost as if he wished to avoid accompanying Marion home.'

We were standing in the drawing-room as I spoke. Suddenly I gave a start as my eye drifted to the mantelpiece. 'What an extraordinary coincidence!' I exclaimed. A strange eerie feeling came over me. Marion's lost photo had been restored to its frame.

CHAPTER XII

William resumes his story: I am now aware that I should not have invoked the aid of Elizabeth. A man should work out his own destiny. Once a woman precipitates herself in an affair, complications are bound to follow. Also Elizabeth is no ordinary woman. There are times when I question whether she is human. Was it not her idea that I should - but I must try to chronicle the events in their correct sequence.

The mistake I made primarily, was in not going away directly I first heard from Elizabeth of Miss Warrington's unfortunate and misplaced attachment for me. Things might then have adjusted themselves quite naturally. The idea, however, of a sensitive woman suffering on my account was exceedingly distasteful to me. If, I decided, I could bring about her complete disillusionment my conscience would be at rest. Also there would then be no necessity to cut myself off from the Warringtons, and give up my pleasant discourses with Henry. Thus, I felt, I was taking the most advisable course under the circumstances.

As for Miss Warrington herself, her behaviour was so inexplicable I wondered if her mind was not beginning to get unhinged. In the first place it was, I thought, unmaidenly enough that she should, through the medium of Elizabeth, thrust her photo on me; but that the photo should be accompanied by some feeble selection from the ill-balanced outpourings of Byron (who is my pet aversion) was, indeed, almost revolting.

Further, her attitude towards me in the presence of others was one of open hostility. So well, indeed, did she act on one occasion when I happened to be dining at her brother's house, that a new hope sprang up within me. I began to think that her strange uncalled-for passion for me had passed - in short, that her love had turned to hate. So impressed was I with this idea that when I next called at the Warringtons' I asked Elizabeth if I could speak to her alone for a few moments.

'About Miss Marryun, I'll bet,' she remarked. Looking at her I thought she accompanied her words with a slight lowering of the left eyelid. I trust I was mistaken. Free as the girl is in her speech I have never given her any encouragement to embellish it by winking.

'Naturally, the subject has been preying on my mind,' I admitted. 'But I am not so tortured with misgivings as before. Miss Warrington has ceased to - er - interest herself in me. In fact she detests me.'

'Oo ses that tom-my-rot?' asked the girl, turning on me almost fiercely.

'Miss Warrington was so excessively rude and abrupt in her manner to me the other evening,' I explained, 'that I am now convinced she has suddenly grown to hate me.'

'If you're not as blind as a bat!' commented Elizabeth. 'Can't you see she's doin' that to 'ide 'er feelings - so that you'll never guess 'ow 'er 'eart is torn an' bleedin' like.'

'Dear me, Elizabeth, do you mean this?' I asked in the utmost concern.

'Sure of it. As a matter o' fact she's more gone on you than ever. She's got to not eatin' now, so you can guess 'ow bad she is.'

I wiped the gathering moisture from my brow. 'Elizabeth, this is terrible - it must be stopped. I must discover some way to make Miss Warrington actually dislike me. In this I hope for your assistance. You know Miss Warrington much better than I do. You are, no doubt, acquainted with her likes and prejudices?'

'Not 'arf, I aint,' she said.

Taking this as meaning an affirmative, I continued, 'Perhaps you are able to tell me what it is about me that attracts her. I have a plan - I shall do exactly the opposite of what she desires of me.'

'To set her agen you, like,' remarked Elizabeth.

'Exactly.'

She stood for a few moments regarding me with her head on one side. Had you known her to be capable of it you might almost have imagined that she was thinking. Certainly she breathed much harder than usual. At last, to my profound astonishment, she suddenly sat down, threw her apron over her face and burst into unrestrained laughter.

'Compose yourself, my good girl,' I said, anxious lest the family should overhear, 'what is the matter?'

'I got an idea,' she said as soon as she had recovered. 'It aint 'arf a bad one. You say you want to know wot it is Miss Marryun likes about you?'

'I do, indeed,' I said eagerly.

'Well, I can tell you that right away. It's your towsled look, so to speak. Only the other day she ses to me, she ses, "Wot I like about Mr. Roarings is the rough kind o' suits 'e wears, them baggy trousis, an' also 'is great clompin' boots. I like the free an' easy way 'e throws 'is feet up to the ledge of the mantel-piece," she ses, "an' the way 'e 'as of wearin' 'is 'air 'anging all

Florence A. Kilpatrick

about 'is ears, shaggy-like."'

'Incredible!' I exclaimed.

'An' only yesterday she stood on this very spot where you are now and ses to me, thoughtful like: "Don't you love a man with a heavy beard an' moustarch - like Mr. Roarings, f r instance?" she ses.'

'"Well, miss, since you put the question to me," I ses plain out; "I'm not parshul to either, though I've 'ad young men with 'em, singly and both together. I prefers 'em entirely without, but beggars can't be choosers, can they?"'

'Then Miss Marryun said thoughtful like: "I think I'm rather different from other wimmin, Elizabeth. Very few would admire a man like Mr. Roarings. But 'e's my style, so to speak, if I was pickin' an' choosin'. But to show you 'ow strange I am," she goes on, "if 'e made 'isself spruce I should get to dislike 'im all at once."'

I raised my head sharply, suffused by a glow of hope. 'Elizabeth, my good girl,' I exclaimed, 'is it so easy to accomplish as all that?'

'I'm not so sure about easy,' she commented, looking me over as if I'd been an unlabelled exhibit in a Zoo. '"Rome wasn't built in a day," as the sayin' is, but it's a long lane that 'as no turnin'. "If 'e," ses Miss Marryun, meanin' you, "was got up real smart with a fancy westcoat, a crease down the front of 'is trousis, shinin' button boots, and wos to shave orf 'is beard and moustarch - " she said that bit very earnest, too - "well, I should fair detest the sight of 'im."'

I sank down in a seat with a groan of despair. Elizabeth was right. Such a metamorphosis would not be easy. It would mean the overturning of my most cherished convictions, an upheaval of the very routine of my existence. Would life be worth living if one awoke in a morning to the knowledge of the rites that every day would bring forth? A matutinal shave, trousers to be taken from the press, collars and cuffs to be changed, hair and nails to be trimmed, the two latter, if not every day, at all events occurring with enough frequency to keep a simple man in a constant state of unrest.

'Elizabeth,' I said, shuddering, 'I cannot do all this.'

'Oo's arskin' you to?' demanded the girl. 'I was only repeating wot Miss Marryun ses to me with 'er own lips. "Yes, I should fair get to detest 'im if 'e was spruce," was 'er very words.'

I pondered. 'Are you quite sure she stipulated about the beard?'

'She did that. She mentioned it pertickler three times.'

I shook my head firmly. Whatever happened I did not mean to concede that point. My beard is one of my best friends. By allowing it to grow to a suitable length it conceals the fact when my ties have grown shabby, and saves me any unnecessary changing of collars. No, I would never be clean-shaven. I could not face the world stripped of my natural facial coverings.

'There may be something in what you say, and I will consider your suggestion regarding the trousers, Elizabeth,' I conceded, 'but the suggestion that I should shave is perfectly monstrous and I won't think of it for a moment.'

'Well, to my mind it's one of the first things wot ought to be done with you,' she said in what seemed to me a disparaging sort of voice, 'wots the good o' puttin' a fancy westcoat an' a watch an' albert on a chap when 'e's got an 'ead like a wild man o' the woods. There ort to be no 'arf an' 'arf about it, I ses.'

I looked at the girl sternly, feeling that her speech was becoming unduly familiar. Nevertheless, I was conscious of a certain gratitude for her suggestion, and after she had gone out, I began to consider it from all points. There could be no harm in gradually making those changes in my habits and apparel which would bring about Miss Warrington's disillusionment, but it must be fairly gradual. Otherwise it might attract undue attention, for there are times when I think I am just a trifle careless about my appearance.

I decided I had better begin operations with a new suit. This would involve changing my regular tailor. The one who has had my custom for the last quarter of a century is used to my way of putting my head round his door once in three years and commanding, 'A tweed lounge suit, the same as the last.'

'Yes, sir,' he invariably concurs, 'any difference in measurements, sir?'

'I think not,' I reply, 'but make it quite loose and comfortable in case I've added a few inches to the waist.'

That is all. Occasionally, of course, I vary the order by making it an overcoat, or an extra pair of slacks (when I burn holes in my usual ones, which frequently happens), but the procedure is always the same. It can easily be understood that I had not the courage to confront him after all these years with a demand for the latest thing in the season's suitings, and especial injunctions regarding style and cut.

As I was dwelling on the annoyances and difficulties that were already presenting themselves, Miss Warrington came in. I must confess that, as I looked at the irritating female whose misplaced affections were already harassing me, I felt slightly confused. Since I had first learned of her insane infatuation I had studiously avoided being left alone with her for one instant. At the moment, however, there was no possibility of escape, as she stood between me and the door, thus effectively barring my exit. I could only confront her uneasily, trying to avoid her direct gaze and, as I did so, I could not help remarking that she, too, was obviously embarrassed.

Then, as if taking a resolution, she came up to me and looked me squarely in the face. I moved away, a faint shiver of apprehension going down my spine.

'Mr. Rawlings,' she said slowly and impressively, 'there is one thing I want to say regarding your conduct. When you are addressing photographs, may I ask you to do it with lowered voice, or at all events in a purely conversational tone?' Then she swept out of the room, banging the door behind her.

As for me, I was left dazed and struggling to grasp the strange import of her mystic words. Why this constant reference to the photograph she had so shamelessly thrust upon me, and which, as a direct hint to her that I did not desire it, I had replaced in its frame at the first opportunity?

What had come over the woman? I began to be more than ever convinced of my former suspicion that her fatal and erratic passion for myself was beginning to unhinge her mind. I saw that I must lose no time in bringing about her disillusionment.

CHAPTER XIII

'Henry, do you think William has been looking particularly unhappy lately?' I inquired.

Henry grunted. Converted for the moment into 'A Well-known Actor,' he was digging amongst his theatrical cuttings for reminiscent purposes, and was, therefore, somewhat abstracted.

I, too, was supposed to be working, but try as I would I could not help thinking of William. I felt sorry for him - he looked so distrait. When, as he vaguely hinted, he had conceived an attachment for me I did not think it was likely to cause him any unhappiness. Indeed, I never imagined him capable of feeling any emotions but those of a purely physical character - such as the effects of cold, heat, hunger or bodily pain. And here he was, sighing and looking so dejected it was depressing even to see him about the place. I had just been re-reading *Cyrano de Bergerac*, whose case seemed rather applicable to William. Could it be possible that under his rough exterior the poor fellow had all the sentiment and fiery imagination of Cyrano, and suffered the same sensitive torment about his appearance. Did William, like Cyrano, shudder when his eye rested even on his own shadow? Did he feel that because of his physical failings the love of woman must be for ever denied him?

I must admit that William was a trifle more interesting to me now than he had previously been. Every woman finds something rather gratifying in being worshipped from afar, even if it is by an 'impossible.' Yet the idea of making him unhappy was distasteful to me. I repeated my question to Henry.

'Never seen William unhappy yet,' replied Henry, looking up, 'he's one of those few chaps who seem contented with life - only wish I was the same.'

Something in his tone made me promptly forget William and concentrate on Henry. 'Aren't you contented?' I asked.

He paused a moment before replying, and then rather wearily indicated the article he was writing. 'It's this kind of thing, you know - where does it all lead to? At times I think journalism is the most exacting profession in the world.'

'What do you mean?' I asked, puzzled at his tone.

'It is exacting because it seems to lead to nothing,' he continued. 'For instance, just think of all the energy, brains and effort involved in the bringing out of a newspaper. Yet it is only read casually, skimmed over by most people, then tossed on one side and instantly forgotten. It is conceived, born, and it dies all in one day. Do you ever see any one reading a morning paper at, say, four o'clock in the afternoon? It is hopelessly out of date by that time.'

'I hadn't thought of it like that,' I pondered. 'Of course, journalism isn't like a business that you can build up and constantly improve; but you can at least establish a reputation amongst newspaper readers.'

'You can't do that so well nowadays,' returned Henry, who seemed in pessimistic vein, 'owing to the present demand for getting well-known names attached to articles. We write them all the same, of course, but it's the people with the well-known names that get the credit for having a good literary style. Well, I always put the best of myself into my work - I can't write

Florence A. Kilpatrick

anything in a hasty, slovenly manner - but where does it lead to? Some day, perhaps, my ideas will give out and then -' he made a little hopeless gesture.

He was silent a moment, staring out of the window. 'Then there's another thing,' he went on, 'this constant grind leaves me no time to get on with my play. If I could only get it finished it might bring me success - even fame. But how shall I ever get the leisure to complete it?'

A feeling of compunction swept over me. I went up to him and put my hand on his shoulder. 'Henry, dear old chap, I never thought you felt like this about things.' Certainly he was writing a play, but as he had been engaged on it now for over ten years (Henry is a conscientious writer), my interest in it was not so keen as it had been when he first told me of the idea a decade previously.

'Couldn't you do a little of your play every evening after dinner?' I suggested.

'I'm too brain weary by that time - my ideas seem to have given out. Sometimes I think I must renounce the notion of going on with it - and it's been one of my greatest ambitions.'

I smoothed his hair tenderly, noticing how heavily flecked it was with grey and how it silvered at the temples. Poor Henry, he reminded me just then of *L'homme a la cervelle d'or*, a fantastic story of Daudet's, where he tells of a man possessed of a brain of gold which he tore out, atom by atom, to buy gifts for the woman he loved until, in the end (she being an extravagant type), he was left without a scrap of brain to call his own and so expired. The man was, of course, supposed to be a writer, and the brain of gold his ideas. It made me feel quite uneasy to think that Henry, too, might be, metaphorically speaking, steadily divesting himself of brain day by day in order to support The Kid and me in comfort.

'I ought not to grumble,' he said at last. 'Very few people can do what they want to in this world. Take you, my dear, for instance. You are not following your natural bent when you write those articles for the Woman's Page.'

'I should hope not - I loathe 'em,' I said viciously.

'There's one thing about it,' he went on musingly, 'we'll see that The Kid has every chance when she grows up.'

We are looking forward very much to the time when The Kid will be grown up. Henry says he pictures her moving silently about the house, tall, graceful, helpful, smoothing his brow when he is wearied, keeping his papers in order, correcting his proofs and doing all his typing for him. I, too, for my part, have visions of her taking all household cares off my shoulders, mending, cooking, making my blouses and her own clothes, and playing Beethoven to us in the evenings when our work is done. In her spare time we anticipate that she will write books and plays that will make her famous.

We have visions of these things, I repeat - generally when The Kid is in bed asleep with her hands folded on her breast in a devotional attitude, a cherubic smile on her lips. There are, however, other times when I hope for nothing more exacting than the day to come when she will keep herself clean.

I often wonder where all the stickiness comes from that she manages to communicate from her person to the handles of doors, backs of chairs and other such places where you are most likely to set your hand unconsciously. Henry has a theory about it oozing from the pores of her skin, and says she conceals some inexhaustible sources of grime which is constantly rising to the surface. In which case you can't entirely blame The Kid.

Under the circumstances, however, we feel that she ought to practise more restraint. Always when she is most thickly coated in dirt and varnished with the glutinous substance already referred to, does she most strongly feel the calls of affection.

Then is the moment when she flings her arms about Henry and presses long kisses on his clean collar, or gently caresses the entire surface of my new blouse. Nothing, I have remarked, can stir her demonstrative nature so much as the sight of Henry and me arrayed in all the glory of evening attire. The merest glimpse of my georgette theatre gown, or the chaste folds of Henry's tie, scintillating collar and shirt front send her flying to us with hands that fondle and lips that cling. If we repel her and compromise by kissing the middle of her head, she has a way of giving us haunting looks that, after we have sallied forth to the halls of pleasure, can make us feel uncomfortable for the entire evening.

'Yes, when The Kid is grown up,' Henry went on, 'perhaps she'll have the success that has been denied to us, old girl.'

I was about to reply when my attention was arrested by a confused murmur of voices in the hall. I distinguished Elizabeth's, and as the other was a man's tones, I supposed she was having a little badinage at the side door with one of the tradesmen, as is her wont. As in time it did not die away, but began to get a little more heated (one voice appearing to be raised in entreaty and the other, Elizabeth's, in protest), I thought I had better saunter out and interrupt the causerie. Elizabeth has occasionally to be reminded of her work in this manner. She is too fond of gossiping.

I opened the door ostentatiously and sallied out - just in time to see Elizabeth playfully pulling William by the beard. 'You get them whiskers orf - narsty, rarspin' things,' she was saying.

It was an awful moment. Elizabeth had the grace to look ashamed of herself for once, and drifted back to her sink without a word. As for William, he appeared thoroughly unnerved. He tottered towards me. 'Let me explain,' he began.

'William!' I said in stern tones. Then again, '*William!*' He wilted under my gaze. 'I should never have thought such a thing of you,' I continued.

He pointed with a finger that trembled in the direction of the kitchen. 'That girl has no respect for any one or anything in the world. Traditions, class distinctions are as nothing to her. She would put out her tongue at Homer.'

'Or pull the beard of William,' I added sarcastically.

'Until I met her,' he went on fiercely, 'I was entirely a democrat. But now I see that once power gets into the hands of the common people we are damned!'

'But what has all this to do with your flirting with Elizabeth?' I demanded.

He seemed so overcome at this very natural comment on my part that for a moment I thought he was going to have a seizure of some sort. 'I - I - *flirt*, and with Elizabeth?' he repeated when he had slightly recovered himself. 'Madame, what do you mean to insinuate?'

He drew himself up to his full height of six feet three, and, looking at him as he towered above me with his mane of disordered hair and flowing beard, I could not help thinking he rather resembled Samson in one of his peevish moods. The indignation that possessed him seemed sincere enough, but the circumstances of the case utterly bewildered me. I was gazing at him in perplexity when Henry came out of the study.

'What's all this parleying in the hall, noise without, voices heard "off," and so forth?' he demanded.

William gave me such an agonized look of entreaty I decided I would say nothing about what had just occurred. 'It is only I endeavouring to get our friend William to rub his feet on the mat,' I retorted cheerfully. 'But let us go into the consulting chamber.'

William followed me into the study and took his usual seat at the fireside in a dejected manner. Then went through a strange gymnastic.

He had just started to swing his feet up to the mantelpiece when he paused with them in mid-air and brought them down again. The arrested action had a droll effect.

'Have a smoke,' said Henry, pretending not to notice this peculiar conduct and pushing the tobacco jar towards him.

'No thanks, old man,' he replied. 'I'm giving up smoking - for a time.'

It was now Henry's turn to look surprised. 'Giving up smoking,' he ejaculated. 'What's wrong - is it your liver?'

'No, no, my liver's all right.'

'Your lungs, then?'

'Of course, not.'

'It surely can't be your heart?'

William began to look annoyed. 'Look here, can't I go without a smoke for once without my entire anatomy being held up for discussion?' He then produced a cigarette and proceeded to light it.

'I thought you'd given up smoking,' commented the puzzled Henry.

'Do you call this smoking?' he replied in disgust. 'You might as well give lemonade to a man who asks for a brandy and soda and tell him it's just as good.'

'Then why renounce your pipe at all?' asked Henry, still mystified.

'I've decided to go through a sort of mental training,' replied

William, speaking rather quickly and avoiding my eye. 'I think a man has no right to become the slave of habit. Directly he feels he is dropping into a groove he ought to face about and go in exactly the opposite direction.'

'Is that what you're doing just now?' I asked, wondering if this was an explanation of the Elizabeth episode.

'Exactly. It is the only way to build up one's character. Now, some people might think me a little careless regarding dress.'

'The ultra-fastidious might consider you a trifle insouciant, William.'

'That is one of the points in my character I intend to correct.' He dived into his pocket as he spoke and produced a brown paper parcel. William can carry any number of things in his pockets without making his figure look any bulgier or more unsymmetrical than usual. He boasts that he has at times gone on a three weeks' walking tour with all the luggage he required for that period disposed about his person, his damp sponge (concealed in the crown of his hat) keeping his head delightfully cool in the heat of the day.

'What have you got there, William?' I inquired as he unfolded the parcel.

'My first step in the evolution of character,' he replied solemnly, and took out a pair of white spats, and some fawn-coloured gloves.

'You don't mean you're going to wear those?' gasped Henry.

'I am - abhorrent as they are to me,' rejoined William mournfully.

'You may call it building up character if you like,' said Henry shortly, 'but I call it a lot of damned rot.' He pulled hard at his cigar, and then added, 'You're suffering from softening of the brain, my boy, or something of the sort.'

William looked at me in questioning despair, and in that moment my heart softened towards him. In a flash I understood. He had so often heard me urge Henry to wear white spats and light-coloured gloves, though all my coercion and entreaty had been in vain. William had thought by donning these things - which on him would have a grotesque effect - he would win my favour. Poor fellow! I was quite touched by his devotion, his absolutely hopeless passion.

'These things wouldn't be in keeping with the rest of you,' I said gently; 'they require to be accompanied by all the - er - appurtenances of the smart man.'

'Is - is - a beard an appurtenance?' he asked in a hollow voice.

'Not an appurtenance, William - perhaps a detriment would be the better word.'

He emitted a sound that was half a groan. 'I knew it,' he said. 'Well, what must be, must be, I suppose.'

'You're getting profound,' snorted Henry, who apparently objected to William in his present mood; and he proceeded to distract his attention by touching on a recent stirring debate in the House. William allowed Henry to talk on unchecked - your man who indulges in argument abhors that - and left unusually early for him.

'That fellow is undoubtedly going off his head,' commented Henry after his departure. 'I wonder what's wrong with him.'

I smiled rather sadly, and mentally decided that I must cure William of his infatuation for me without delay.

CHAPTER XIV

It is not easy to write - even on such a simple topic as 'How to Retain a Husband's Love' - if your attention is being distracted by a conscientious rendering of Czerny's 101 Exercises in an adjoining room. I could get no further with my article than the opening lines (they like an introductory couplet on the Woman's Page): -

It is the little rift within the lute
That by and by will make the music mute!

whereas The Kid, having disposed of all the major and minor scales and a goodly slice of Czerny, had now started her 'piece,' 'The Blue Bells of Scotland.' It was too much. I flung down my pencil and strode to the door. 'Moira,' I shrieked, 'stop that practising instantly.'

'Yes, Mama, dear.'

'Don't you understand I'm writing and want to be quiet?'

'Yes, Mama, dear. May I go on when you've finished writing?'

'I suppose so; but when I've quite finished it will be about your bedtime,' I said, trying not to feel exasperated.

'Then, may I get up an hour earlier in the morning to practise, Mama, dear?'

Florence A. Kilpatrick

There is something almost unnatural in the way that child fights her way through all obstacles to the piano and the monotony of Czerny. All the other parents in the world seem to be bewailing the fact that they can't get their children to practise. I know I ought to be proud and glad that The Kid is so bent upon a musical career, but even as the lion and the lamb cannot lie down together, neither can a writer and an incipient musician dwell in the same house in amity.

Through almost illimitable difficulties (for when at work Henry can no more stand piano practice than I can) The Kid has got to the Variations of 'The Blue Bells of Scotland.' Nevertheless she is yearning for the day when she will arrive at the part where she crosses hands (Var. 8) - a tremendous achievement in her eyes, but viewed with cold aloofness by Henry and me.

As I returned to my writing Henry entered the room.

'Will you as a Scotsman tell me,' I inquired before he could speak, 'what English people have done that they should be so unduly annoyed by the bells of Scotland, why those bells should be blue, and who was responsible for bringing the said blue bells (with variations) across the Border?'

'I see The Kid's been annoying you again,' he commented. 'It's a pity she gets no chance of practising.'

I looked at him sternly. 'No chance! On the contrary, she never lets a chance escape her. I think it's the fierce Northern strain she inherits from you, Henry, that makes her so persistent. She reminds me of Bannockburn -'

'Bannockburn!' ejaculated Henry.

'King Bruce and the Spider and all that, you know. Didn't he go on trying and trying until he succeeded? That's what The Kid does with her scales. I think I understand why in 1603 we put a Scotch King on the English throne - you wouldn't have given us any peace if we hadn't.'

'Well, don't blame me for it, my dear,' replied Henry. 'I dropped in to tell you that William has just 'phoned up to say he accepts our invitation to dinner this evening, but he is most anxious to know who else is coming.'

I stared. 'This is most unusual. What should it matter to him who is coming?'

'I told him, of course, that there was only Marion and ourselves, and then he asked if he should get into evening dress. What do you think of that?' We looked at each other in silent amazement.

'William - in - evening - dress,' I echoed blankly. 'What can it mean?'

'Frankly, I think the poor old chap's brain is getting a little unhinged,' hazarded Henry. 'Do you remember the episode with the white spats and gloves the other day? I think you ought to persuade him to see a specialist, my dear.'

Suddenly I remembered the apparent reason for poor William's altered manner and smiled. 'I don't think we need call in medical aid just yet,' I replied.

Nevertheless, I felt that he must be cured of this foolishness as soon as possible, for, as I had already hinted to him, any attempt at embellishing his person would only make him appear more grotesque. How little did I then dream of the amazing surprise that was in store for me!

I was sitting alone in the drawing-room that same evening awaiting my two guests, Marion and William (Henry was upstairs dressing), when Elizabeth burst into the room.

'Oh, 'm, 'e's come!' she exclaimed, 'an' you never did see anything in your life 'arf so funny. I've been larfin' fit to split my sides.'

'Elizabeth,' I said coldly, 'what is wrong? Of whom are you speaking?'

For answer she threw her apron over her head and went off into an almost hysterical fit of laughing.

''Oo'd have thort it,' she said when she had slightly recovered. 'That there grizzly bear of a Mr. Roarings, too!'

'So you are referring to one of my guests,' I interrupted sternly. 'I'm ashamed of you, Elizabeth.'

'Well, you only ort ter see 'im now! Talk about grubs turnin' into butterflies -'

'I'm not talking about anything of the sort,' I interposed with extreme asperity of manner. 'Am I to understand that Mr. Rawlings has arrived?'

'Not 'arf, 'e 'asn't. Wait till you see Mamma's boy. 'E's a fair razzle-dazzle from top to toe. Oh, my godmother!' And being seized with another burst of hysterical laughter she dashed from the room.

I sighed as I put aside the French novel I had been reading when I was so rudely disturbed. I could not help wishing just then that Elizabeth had a little less character and a little more deference, and I decided that I must rebuke her for her familiarity. Then, remembering her supreme art in grilling a steak, I decided that rebukes - practised on domestics - are rather risky things in these days.

'Good evening,' said the deep voice of William behind me.

'Good evening,' I said casually, turning round and holding out my hand. Then I started back, my hand falling limply to my side. It was William who stood before me, because I recognized his voice - but that was all I recognized at the moment. Not a shred of his former self seemed to have remained.

I think I have, from time to time, represented William as shabby, bulky, shapeless, hairy, and altogether impossible as far as appearance goes. Can any words depict my astonishment at seeing him so suddenly transformed, glorified, redeemed and clean-shaven? His figure, which once appeared so stodgy, now looked merely strong and athletic encased in a well-fitting morning coat, a waistcoat of a discreet shade of smoke grey, with a hint of starched pique slip at the opening. His irreproachable trousers were correctly creased - not too marked to be ostentatious, but just a graceful fold emerging, as it were, out of the texture, even as the faint line of dawn strikes across the darkened sky.

But it was his head that attracted me most. There was no denying it - shorn of his overgrowth of whiskers and put into a correct setting, William was handsome; even more than that, he was interesting. He had that firm, chiselled kind of mouth which women and artists find so attractive, and a delightful cleft in his chin; his hair, which had hitherto always struck me as being so unkempt and disordered, now that it was brushed smoothly back from his brow and curled into the nape of his neck gave him a distinguished appearance. I directed one long look at him and then instinctively dived to the mirror.

'Oh, William,' I gasped, 'is it possible?'

'Is what possible?' he inquired.

'Why just think of it,' I replied, groping in my pocket for my powder puff. '*You're a man!*'

'What else should I be?' he asked, apparently mystified.

'You used to be - just William. But now,' I sidled up to him, 'you've changed amazingly.'

'Yes, I know that,' he growled with some of his former gruffness of manner. 'Can you imagine what a tremendous amount of determination and will power I required to get myself up like this?'

'And a good tailor as well - don't forget that,' I added, running an appraising eye over his form. 'I must get his address for Henry. Yes, it was brave of you. What made you do it, William?'

He avoided my eye and looked embarrassed. 'I had an object, of course. Didn't I explain the other evening -'

'I remember. You did say something about a man not getting into a groove.' I smiled, feeling slightly self-conscious for a moment. 'And how do you feel now you're entirely metamorphosed?'

'Entirely metamorphosed, am I?' he said rather bitterly, 'Just on account of a change of raiment. Yet Dr. Johnson said, "Fine clothes are good only as they supply the want of other means of procuring respect."'

'Oh, I always respected you, William,' I put in hastily, 'And don't quote Dr. Johnson now. It doesn't go with your tie.'

He groaned. 'Must I change my expressions, my thoughts, my very mode of living to match the garments I wear?'

'I'm afraid you must. But tell me,' I added, looking earnestly into his face, 'doesn't this outward change affect you inwardly as well - just a little? You *must* be feeling more - what shall I say - sprightly than before?'

He looked down at me as if puzzled, and then said in a half shame-faced way, 'Mrs. Warrington, there is some truth in that remark of yours. Some subtle, inexplicable change that I cannot account for has come over me. Even as Samson's strength lay in his hair, do you think my reason lay in my beard?'

'It depends on the quality of the reason. Describe your present symptoms to me, William.'

He avoided my gaze. 'It is quite impossible to analyse them, I assure you.'

'Let me help. Look at me steadily,' I said impressively. 'Now try, as far as possible, to describe me.'

There was a pause. 'I'm afraid you'll be offended, Madame,' he began.

'No, I won't. Go on,' I commanded.

'Well, as a matter of fact, although I have known you for over nine years, it has never before occurred to me to notice that you are an - an - exceedingly pretty woman - but I am offending you?'

'Not in the least, William. Go on.'

'Before, I merely remarked you as Henry's wife - that was all. Why should I so suddenly observe your facial aspect? As Dr. Johnson once said -'

'Cut out Dr. Johnson, and go on with that bit about the facial aspect,' I put in gently.

'It must, of course, be self-consciousness arising out of my unusual adornment,' he went on, 'but despite myself I am compelled to notice your attractive qualities. I must, however, overcome this deplorable tendency - combat it -'

'I shouldn't combat it too strongly at first,' I suggested. 'It's always better to do things by degrees. What a nice mouth you have, William.'

'So have you,' he said, pondering on the discovery.

I blushed. William suddenly started back and smote his brow with his hand. 'Isn't Henry coming in? Where is he?' he demanded wildly.

'Are you so anxious to see Henry at the moment?'

'I am. Mrs. Warrington, I am ashamed to admit the preposterous idea that came into my mind just now. You and Henry would never forgive me - never countenance me again - it was intolerable, incredible -' He paused and wiped his brow. 'Why doesn't Henry come in?'

'What was the preposterous idea?' I asked, wondering.

'Well, you'll hardly believe it - scarcely realize what you've escaped . . . just now, had you been a foot closer to me I believe - I believe, Mrs. Warrington, I should have kissed you!'

I moved a step nearer to him. 'William, I should never have forgiven you if you had,' I said, raising my face to his so that he could see how intensely earnest I was.

The door opened, and Henry and Marion came in together.

'Netta!' exclaimed Marion, 'how could you!'

'My dear,' remarked Henry, 'I am surprised. How is it I come in and find a man kissing you?'

'I don't know, Henry,' I replied meekly, 'unless it's because that door opens so quietly!'

CHAPTER XV

An exclamation from William made us all turn and look at him.

'I must have been mad,' he groaned, sinking into a chair and covering his face with his hands.

'That's what I thought myself just now when I caught sight of your waistcoat,' said Henry, staring at him. 'What is the meaning of all this - why the flawless trousers, the immaculate morning coat?'

'I - I - put on a morning coat because you said I wasn't to get into evening dress,' he replied. 'I know it isn't the correct thing for dinner, but you've only yourself to blame.'

Henry continued to stare at him. 'I was quite right. Your brain is unhinged, William. When I last saw you, you appeared fairly normal - and now I come in and discover you arrayed like the lilies of the field and kissing my wife.'

William gave a cry like a wounded animal. 'Your indictment is only too true. Henry, it is terrible. I can never even hope for your forgiveness for such a heinous offence. The only reparation I can make is to go forth from your house, shake from my feet the dust of your hospitable roof -'

'That metaphor's wrong, William,' I interposed.

'- and pass out of your lives for ever.'

'What on earth are you talking about, old chap?' inquired Henry.

'Have I not betrayed the trust you always reposed in me?'

'I wouldn't put it as strong as that,' replied Henry, eyeing him up and down, 'though you certainly have made a bit of a guy of yourself. Who created those trousers?'

'I - I - was not referring to my change of apparel, Henry, but to that most unfortunate aberration on my part, when I was impelled by some strange uncontrollable impulse to bestow a labial salute on your wife. Heaven only knows that I -'

'As for that, I expect she egged you on,' calmly rejoined that horrid Henry. 'I know her. You did flirt with him, didn't you, Netta?'

Before I could reply William sprang to his feet and placed himself before me. 'Stop, Henry!' he exclaimed, 'You have no right to suggest such a thing. If I took a gentle unsuspecting woman unawares, then I am willing to stand by the consequences of my rash act. Never for one moment, I can assure you, did such a thought enter Mrs. Warrington's head. She was wholly unprepared -'

'I'm not so sure of that,' put in Marion, with a sniff.

I began to feel somewhat of a martyr. 'Yes, it *was* rather a surprise,' I remarked.

'Only a moment before,' continued William, 'Mrs. Warrington had said to me, "If you do kiss me, I shall never forgive you!"' Oh, clumsy, clumsy William!

'Then you had been discussing it,' commented Marion, who seemed unusually chilly about the innocent affair.

'Well, I'm hungry, so let's have dinner now,' suggested Henry, 'and we can settle the discussion afterwards.'

But William strode to the door. 'No, no, Henry, I cannot break bread in your house again after this distressing incident. I have imposed on your kindness and good faith, disturbed your trust in me -'

'Well, I forgive you this time if you promise never to bestow any of those, what d'ye call 'em - labial salutes on Netta again. Now let's have dinner.'

'No, no, old man, you may forgive me, but I shall never forgive myself.'

Henry began to look irritated. 'For Heaven's sake, Netta, tell him the truth and admit it was your fault, or we shall never get anything to eat to-night.'

I sighed, and going up to William gently pulled back his retreating form by the coat tails. 'You are young, Father William,' I said, 'and innocent in the wiles of women. You've only been born a few hours as far as they are concerned - I don't think it's quite safe for you to go about without your beard just yet. I will tell you nothing but the truth. I incited you to kiss me.'

'I knew it!' snapped Marion.

'Henry, as you see, has treated me under the First Offenders Act and forgiven me. And now, William, I will kiss you once again (with Henry's full consent) for your youth and innocence.' And I suited the action to the word. 'So will Marion, won't you, dear?'

At this William started as if shot. 'Never, never!' he exclaimed, staring at Marion with a hunted look, 'it would be preposterous - infamous.'

The situation was decidedly awkward, especially as Marion, going suddenly pale, gave a little hysterical sort of cry and ran out of the room.

The meal that followed was a silent one. Marion did not speak at all, and when she was not casting furtive glances in William's direction, kept her gaze fixed on her plate. William was monosyllabic, partly, I gathered, on account of recent events, and partly because one of his patent leather boots was obviously causing him anguish. I noticed that he occasionally lifted his foot (as an animal raises a wounded paw) and then set it down again with a sort of half moan.

For one reason I was rather grateful that my guests were so abstracted. That reason was Elizabeth. Her behaviour during dinner, to put it mildly, was disturbing and abnormal. Every time she entered the room to change the plates or hand round the dishes she went through remarkable pantomimic gestures behind the unconscious William's back. She drew my attention to him by nods, winks, and significant gestures. Once or twice she was impelled to clap her hand over her mouth and dash from the room in a spasm of uncontrollable mirth. It was most unnerving; and what with William's gloomy looks, Marion's abstraction, and my constant fear that Elizabeth would spill gravy, custard or something of an equally clinging character, over William during her contortions behind him, I was relieved when the meal was ended.

William at once retired to the study with Henry, presumably for a chat, but chiefly, as I afterwards discovered, to remove his right boot for an hour's respite. He left early, limping heavily.

'It is really most curious about William,' I said to Marion as we sat alone in the drawing-room - Henry having remained in the study to finish some work. 'One can hardly conceive a reason strong enough to induce him to renounce his aboriginal mode of living and become so highly civilized almost in a day.'

Marion lowered her head, and I thought she looked self-conscious. 'A man might do a thing like that for - for love,' she murmured.

I blushed slightly. 'I scarcely think it's more than a passing infatuation.'

'I feel convinced it's stronger than that,' she replied tensely.

'I hope not,' I said in an alarmed tone. 'It would be horrid to see the poor fellow in the throes of a hopeless passion.'

'Perhaps after all it might not be quite hopeless,' rejoined Marion softly.

I raised my head sharply. 'I don't think you are justified in that remark,' I said stiffly, 'what you saw between him and me was only a little harmless fun. As if, indeed, there is any man living who could make me forget dear old Henry for a minute -'

'You!' exclaimed Marion with a start. 'I wasn't thinking of you, Netta.'

'Then who -?'

'I - I - was referring to - myself.' She put down her knitting on her knee and looked at me half defiantly, her cheeks flushed.

'But, my dear Marion, when has he shown you the slightest attention?' I was impelled to remark. 'You have always professed the profoundest contempt for him.'

'Not contempt, Netta. I have remarked that he was untidy.'

'You said the other evening that you considered him to be the last man on earth a woman could like.'

'No doubt, dearest, but that was before I had discovered a woman kissing him.'

'Perhaps you regret it was not yourself in that enviable position, darling?'

'No, my love. I don't think the position of a married woman discovered kissing a man other than her husband *is* enviable; do you?'

Marion's obtuse and unreasonable attitude puzzled me. I am quick tempered, and was about to reply hotly, when the door opened and Elizabeth entered.

'Miss Marryun,' she said, nodding mysteriously in the direction of my sister-in-law, 'I bin lookin' at the cards for you an' I see a warnin' in 'em. You'll 'ave to keep an eye on 'im if you want to keep 'im.'

Marion did not look so mystified as I expected at this unusual outburst. 'Thank you for the warning, Elizabeth,' she said in an affable tone.

'You gotta rival for 'is affeckshuns,' continued Elizabeth.

Marion raised an eyebrow in my direction. 'No doubt,' she commented.

'What is all this nonsense?' I asked, a little testily.

'Elizabeth is, as you know, a fatalist,' explained Marion. 'She places her faith in cards, which, I am repeatedly telling her, is utter nonsense.'

'It aint nonsense,' expostulated Elizabeth in an injured tone. 'You gotta fair rival acrost your parth -'

'I'm glad I'm dark,' I murmured.

'Fair an' false she is,' continued the soothsayer, 'the words of 'er mouth are like 'oney an' -'

'I tell you I consider all this rubbish,' interrupted Marion briskly. 'You would be far better not to believe in such foolish things, Elizabeth. They do you no good.'

Elizabeth retired in some indignation, muttering, 'Well, don't say you wasn't told.'

We sat in strained silence - for it was the first occasion there had been any hint of a tiff between us - and after a time Marion rose to go. When Henry had put on his overcoat to accompany her home she was nowhere to be found. Hearing voices proceeding from the kitchen, I went in that direction. It was then I heard Marion remark in a casual tone - the casualness a little overdone: 'You might let me hear if he says any more about it.'

'Right-o, Miss.'

'And, oh, by the way, Elizabeth, what was that you said about a rival - are you quite sure that she is fair?'

CHAPTER XVI

I should like to begin this chapter by saying it's the unexpected that always happens. As that, however, would be too trite a remark, I will only say that William was the last person on earth I should have suspected of falling in love with Gladys Harringay.

She is, indeed, exceedingly pretty in a fluffy kind of way and most men like to flirt with her, but they do not let their attentions develop into anything serious. Perhaps you know the sort of girl she is. She makes a dead set at every eligible man she meets and concentrates on him to such an extent that he ends by losing interest in her altogether - actually avoiding her, in fact. Man is like that, I've observed. I suppose it's the primitive instinct of the hunter which still lurks in him and makes him desire to stalk down his quarry instead of its stalking him. Gladys didn't seem aware of this supreme fact, and (though she affected the giddy airs of eighteen) she was getting perilously near the age when the country considers a woman is wise and staid enough to vote, yet she still remained unwed.

Never for a moment did it occur to me, when I asked her to dine with us one evening, that she would go for William. Still less did I think that he would take even the faintest interest in such a vapid creature. But, as I wanted to say before, it's the unexpected that always happens.

William was looking unusually nice that evening. His eyes had a far-away, rather haunted expression, due to his wearing sock-suspenders for the first time, but, of course, Gladys didn't know that. He seemed like one of the strong, silent heroes of fiction. I can testify that he was silent - perhaps because Gladys did all the talking - and he looked unusually strong. They sat together most of the evening, and she only left his side to go to the piano to sing one of her 'stock' French chansons. Even then she directed it entirely at William.

> *'Mamman, dites-moi, ce qu'on sent quand on aime*
> *Est-ce plaisir, est-ce tourment?'*

she warbled, rolling her r's and looking so fixedly at William that he seemed quite uneasy - he might, indeed, have been more uneasy had his French been equal to following the words of the song. Modern languages, however, like modern writers, do not appeal to him. They must be as dead as mutton before they can awaken his interest. If you want to see him roused to a perfect frenzy of enthusiasm you should see him arguing with Henry as to the comparative dramatic values of Homeric hexameters and Ionian iambics.

But to return to Gladys - or rather Gladys and William, for they remained inseparable for the remainder of the evening. He even accompanied her home, for I saw him dart forward (in his patent leather boots, too, which demanded slow movement on his part), when she rose to go, and hurry out to act as her escort.

A few days later he called in to see us for the sole purpose of inquiring about her. He pretended he wanted to borrow Ruskin's *Munera Pulveris*, but as he went away without the volume we saw how feeble was that pretext.

'With regard to - er - Miss Harringay,' he began, almost as soon as he arrived, 'I must say I consider her a remarkable young lady.'

'She *is*,' I said grimly.

'Would you believe it,' he went on, addressing himself to Henry, 'she is actually a Dr. Johnson enthusiast.'

'Nonsense!' ejaculated Henry.

'It's a fact. Isn't it unusual in one so young and - er - tender and timid that she recalls Keats' dissertation on woman, "she is like a milk-white lamb that bleats for man's protection."'

'Oh, so she's been bleating, has she?' I said cruelly.

'It makes it all the more astonishing that she should have leanings toward the study of serious literature.'

'Who told you she had?'

'She told me so herself.'

'Do you mean to tell me you believe it?'

He looked puzzled. 'Why should she say that if it isn't true? She could have no object in making such a statement. As a matter of fact, I found out quite by accident, when she unconsciously quoted a passage from the great master.'

I began to see light. So that was why Gladys had come up in such haste the day following her introduction to William to borrow *Johnson's Aphorisms*. Oh, hapless, artless William!

'I see now that you were quite right when you once remarked that you feared you had lost your reason with your beard,' I remarked severely. 'Do let things grow again before it is too late.'

'Let what grow?' he asked.

'Everything. Moustache, beard and general air of fuzziness. It's the best protection you can have, my poor fellow.'

He departed rather abruptly after that, seeming somewhat annoyed. I could not understand what was making him so unusually touchy.

'Surely,' I said to Henry, 'even William isn't so blind as to let himself be taken in by that little noodle of a Gladys.'

'Of course he isn't,' replied Henry vehemently, 'do you think a chap is ever deceived by anything like that? He hates to be pounced on, so to speak. Do you know, my dear, that one of the things that first attracted you to me was your complete indifference to myself.'

'Indeed, Henry?' I said, with lowered eyes and modest mien.

'Yes. If you remember I was editing the *Gazette* at the time I first met you, and although you, as one of my contributors, often came up to the office to see me, we remained for a long time on a purely business footing.'

It is true Henry was an unconscionable time in coming to the point. 'Entirely business-like,' I acquiesced.

'When you called to see me to discuss a gross misstatement in one of your articles (which you refused to acknowledge until I had sent for you to put the matter clearly before you), you did not conduct yourself like so many other girls who came to discuss their work with me. You did not attempt to engage in a mild flirtation, make eyes, bend over me as I glanced through the manuscript -'

'Oh, bad, bad girls,' I murmured. 'Do women behave like that with you, Henry?'

'They *did*, my dear. I am speaking of the time before I was married.'

I smiled. What a comfort it is to have a Scotsman for a husband! He is so solid and reliable regarding the opposite sex.

'You, however, employed none of these wiles,' he continued, 'and were almost studiously cold and business-like. For a long time I thought I should never interest you in myself - in fact, I know I took you very much by surprise when I made you an offer, didn't I?'

'I was rather surprised, Henry,' I said, smiling at his retreating form as he went out of the room. Then I turned to Marion, who happened to be present. 'Why, of course,' I commented, 'that makes it all the more serious about William.'

'What are you talking about?' she asked in a puzzled tone.

'If Henry was deceived so easily -'

'Deceived! Oh, Netta!'

'Well, I mean, dear, I'd decided to marry Henry before the episode of the misstatement in my article he just mentioned. I - I - put the misstatement in on purpose to arouse a controversy between us.'

'Netta, how terrible!'

'Why terrible, Marion? I knew Henry would make an excellent husband. Am I not a suitable wife for him?'

'You are just perfect, dear - but you might have been otherwise.'

'That's exactly what I'm driving at, Marion. Gladys is an "otherwise." If I deceived Henry, how much easier is it for her to deceive William? No, she shan't marry him. He'd be wretched.'

Marion smiled. 'You surely don't think there's anything like that between them?'

'He's drifting that way if some one doesn't stop him.'

Again Marion smiled. 'I tell you it's impossible. He couldn't have got over his passion for me so quickly.'

'His passion for you,' I echoed. 'My dear, what do you mean?'

Marion then laid down her sewing and began to speak. I listened amazed, unable at first to credit what she was saying, though gradually I began to understand many things which had hitherto been obscure.

'It's wonderful to think of his having loved you secretly all this time,' I marvelled; 'yet why should he take Elizabeth into his confidence rather than myself? And why didn't you tell me all this before - it would have made things so much simpler.'

'At first, not being aware how handsome he could be made, I did not care for him and -'

'Do you mean, then, that you no longer dislike him, Marion?'

'On the contrary, dear, I have begun to regard him with - with feelings of warmth.'

'Then all goes well, it seems. Now I shall go and speak to Elizabeth about the affair.'

I thought Elizabeth seemed a little uneasy under my questioning, but she reiterated many times: 'I tell you 'e isn't 'arf gone on Miss Marryun - fair mad about 'er 'e is, but 'e told me not to breathe a word about it to a soul.'

'Well, he's mad about some one else now,' I interposed.

Elizabeth looked unduly startled. 'Oo with? Don't say it's that there Miss 'Arringay 'oo wos a-settin' 'er cap so 'ard at 'im the other night?'

I was a little taken aback. 'Yes, that's about it,' I confessed.

Florence A. Kilpatrick

'Well, upon my soul, the sorcy baggage,' burst out Elizabeth with unexpected wrath, 'such imperence after me workin' an' plannin' the way I 'ave. But she shan't 'ave 'im. Look 'ere, 'm, Miss Marryun is just the one fer 'im. Can't it be brought off like?'

I pondered. 'I'll do my best, Elizabeth. If, as you say, he has formed such a strong attachment to Miss Marion, I should like to see them both happy. You say he was particularly anxious to have her photograph?'

I almost imagined at that moment Elizabeth avoided my eye. 'Very pertickler,' she retorted in a muffled voice.

'Very well, then. I, myself, will restore the photo he replaced. It will be the first step to an understanding between them.'

I left the kitchen smiling complacently, feeling that my latest matrimonial scheme for Marion was going to be the easiest I had ever attempted.

Alas! I was reckoning, as the saying is, without my host. The host in this case was Gladys.

CHAPTER XVII

Everything went wrong with my plans from the first. For instance, Marion, the central figure in the plot, went away suddenly to nurse a sick great-aunt. William now became so engrossed with Gladys that he talked of very little else. Thus Henry and I would have avoided him at this stage, if possible; it was not possible, however, to avoid him. We saw more of him than ever. I will explain why.

William was one of those lovers who are terrified of being over-bold or too confident, lest by their presumption they might alarm the timid object of their affections. He needn't have been afraid of wooing Gladys. She flung herself at his head rather obviously, but he seemed so obtuse she must have found him irritating at times. Thus, instead of calling upon her or asking her to meet him by appointment, or arranging an evening at the theatre and otherwise behaving in a sensible manner, he hung about her house, endeavouring to come upon her 'by chance.' Further, having met her at our place he seemed to be under the impression that she was one of my closest friends, and came to see me every day, judging by the times he 'dropped in' in the obvious anticipation of meeting her. Not finding his quarry, he talked about her to Henry, though I must admit his audience was not always sympathetic.

'I don't believe in interfering in these things,' remarked Henry, one evening, when we were alone, 'but, frankly, I should be really sorry to see good old William throw himself away on that frivolous, stupid little Gladys. They'd be desperately unhappy after being married a week. Couldn't something be said to them, do you think - a hint thrown out from time to time?'

'Throwing hints - or anything else - wouldn't be of the slightest use, Henry. Have you ever met a person in love who would listen to sound advice of the sort? If you want to know how to get yourself intensely unpopular - with two people at least - try intervening in what you consider an unsuitable love match.'

I spoke with feeling, for I had once been implored to use my influence to part a couple who were, to all appearances, acutely incompatible. The job was distasteful to me, and I only undertook it because there is a strain of philanthropy in my nature (though that isn't what the incompatibles called it). My intervention had no effect, of course. They are now married - and quite happy - and neither of them will speak to me any more.

Henry continued to look disturbed. 'If he only knew Gladys,' he said, 'but as things are going at present I'm afraid he'll propose before his eyes are opened.'

I felt troubled. For a day or two I pondered on the distressing affair, but I was resolutely determined not to intervene. Then it was the idea occurred to me. To be frank, it was Elizabeth who actually inspired it. I was giving orders for dinner and was suggesting apple turnovers for a sweet, when she blandly remarked, 'Talkin' o' turnovers, Mr. Roarings is dead gone on that there Miss 'Arringay now, I 'ear.'

'Your hearing does seem unusually good,' I said coldly. Certainly, I had never mentioned the subject to any one but Henry. It was a surprise to discover that I had, at the same time, been mentioning it to Elizabeth as well.

'Nice wife she'd make him,' continued the irrepressible Elizabeth, 'a flipperty-flapperty piece o' goods like 'er.'

'We will have cheese straws after the sweet, Elizabeth,' I said in tones of chill rebuke.

'Right-o, 'm. Well, wot are you goin' to *do* about it?'

'Do about what?'

'Mr. Roarings an' Miss 'Arringay. 'E isn't 'er style as any one could see with 'arf an eye, but 'e's fair blinded just now. Wot an eye-opener it'd be if 'e got to know 'er proper - met 'er frequent, so to speak.'

'I'm afraid I don't quite understand.'

'Well, 'ere's a case in point. My sister-in-law's brother - nice young chap 'e was too - fell in with a girl that wasn't the right one fer 'im - no clarss like, - but 'e wouldn't 'ear a word agen 'er. So my sister-in-law thinks of a plan. She arsks both 'er brother an' the young woman 'e was courtin' to go and spend their 'olidays with 'er at the seaside. Which they did an' - bless yer - wot with seein' 'er every day an' gettin' to know 'er too well 'e soon got sick o' 'er. Why, 'e'd given 'er a black eye afore the week was out. Now if Mr. Roarings and Miss 'Arringay met frequent like that -'

'Elizabeth,' I interposed, 'mind your own business'; and I went out of the kitchen with dignity.

Nevertheless, I was compelled to admit that she had given me an inspiration. That girl, under a rough and unpromising exterior, has fecundity of ideas which astonishes me. Had she been in a higher class in life - or even able to spell - she might have been a regular contributor to the Sunday papers.

'Henry,' I said, hurrying into the study. 'I have got a solution regarding William's entanglement. I am going to invite Gladys to spend a week here with us.'

'How can that help? I don't quite see -'

Florence A. Kilpatrick

'My dear ass, the idea isn't a novel one, but in this case it's excellent. I'll write her a note on the instant and ask her if she'll come, giving as a pretext that I'm feeling lonely in Marion's absence.'

'But why this hurry? Hadn't you better think it over first?'

'If I pause to think it over, Henry, I know I shall decide that I can't tolerate Gladys for an entire week. As it is, I expect she'll drive me stark mad. No, no, let me write while I am in my present frenzy of philanthropy?'

'I suppose,' he reflected, 'William will practically spend the week here, too, when he knows Gladys is coming.'

'Exactly. What about it?'

'I'm thinking of my work,' he grumbled. 'Two people being disillusioned under one roof are sure to create interruptions.'

'They shan't interrupt you. I intend to leave them together as much as possible. How glad I am that Gladys isn't the least bit clever - a week might not be long enough if she were.'

'I'm not sanguine about the idea,' was Henry's comment. 'It might work out all right in books and plays; but in real life its effect is extremely doubtful.'

'Not at all. Elizabeth knew a young man who was devoted to a girl until they spent a holiday together. At the end of the first week he gave her a black eye. What more do you want than that?'

'Nothing,' replied Henry, 'if she was quite satisfied. Do you think William's disillusionment will be as abrupt as all that?'

'I'm hopeful. Now don't talk to me until I've finished my letter to Gladys, which demands effort on my part. It must read as if I really wanted her to come.'

Evidently the letter was effective, for Gladys rang up directly she received it and told me she'd be simply charmed to come and that it was perfectly sweet of me to have her. (I rather thought it was myself.)

She came the next day with an abnormal amount of luggage for such a brief visit. But as I told Henry (who said it looked as though she intended wintering in our abode), I had distinctly stipulated that the invitation was for a week only. I was not at that time aware of the barnacle-like qualities of Gladys.

As I anticipated, William also descended on us when he knew we had Gladys for a visitor. I left them alone together at every opportunity, and for a day or two all went well.

Things might have gone better (for Gladys) if she hadn't attempted to be clever. As a matter of fact she over-reached herself. To this day I believe she ascribes her failure to Dr. Johnson, though she was far more to blame than that good old man. She talks very bitterly against him even now.

You see, knowing William's weakness, she played up to it, but not being clever she hadn't got her subject properly in hand. I know the poor girl worked hard at the *Aphorisms*, but she had exhausted what she knew of those by the end of the first day. She did her best, I will admit, and even took the *Lives of the English Poets* to bed with her and concentrated on them until midnight, while she dipped into *The Vanity of Human Wishes* before breakfast. But it was no use. William discovered her deception rapidly, and it seemed to annoy him unduly. His visits began to fall off, and after Gladys had artlessly remarked to him one day, 'Who is that Mr. Boswell you're always talking about - he must be a great friend of yours. I hope you'll introduce me,' he ceased to come altogether.

He had, in fact, arrived at the stage where Gladys irritated him. So had we. But unlike William we could not get away from her. Her visit had already extended two weeks and was melting into a third, and she gave no hint of returning home. It

　　　　　Florence A. Kilpatrick

wouldn't have been so bad if only she had been quiet, but she is the most restless person I have ever known. She was always running up and down stairs, banging doors, playing fragments on the piano, and dashing into the study to talk to Henry when he was writing.

He is, on the whole, an equable man, but more than once I trembled for the consequences when I saw her go up to him, lean over his shoulder and, snatching at some loose pages of his MS., playfully remark, 'What funny crabbed letters! And what is it all about - something you're inventing to deceive us poor public, I'll be bound. I don't believe a word of what you're writing, so there!'

Henry used to say scorching things about Gladys when we retired at night (the only chance we seemed to have now of being alone was in our bedroom), and would ask me when I meant to tell her to go. I suggested he should tell her himself, and he declared it was not the duty of the host. I replied that it was the first time I'd ever heard it was the duty of the hostess either.

We planned to make little speeches in her presence based on the subject of her departure, and fraught with deep and subtle allusion, but she ignored them. We inquired if her mother did not miss her after such a prolonged absence, and she said they rather liked her to be away from home for a few months in the year, as a change was always good. No doubt it was good for her people, but it was bad for Henry and me.

Then one night Henry revolted. 'If she hasn't gone in another two days,' he informed me, 'I'm going to get rooms at an hotel.'

He spoke as if he meant it, and I was mournfully wondering what I ought to do to get Gladys to go, short of being downright rude, when Elizabeth drifted into the problem.

'If Miss 'Arringay's goin' to stop much longer, I ain't,' she announced. 'She makes too much extry work, an' the sight o' 'er about the place fair riles me.'

I looked wearily at Elizabeth. 'No doubt Miss Harringay will be going soon,' I said with an utter lack of conviction.

Elizabeth approached me, and bending down, said in a hoarse whisper, 'Wot is it - carn't you get rid of 'er?'

I did not reply, feeling it distasteful to discuss my guest with a domestic, though I could not refrain from discussing her with Henry.

'Tell you wot you orter do,' said the fertile Elizabeth, 'send for Miss Marryun to come 'ere unexpected, an' then tell Miss 'Arringay you'll want 'er room.'

'But - but I've got another spare room. Miss Harringay knows that.'

Elizabeth winked: I pretended not to see it, but there was no mistaking the distinct muscular movement of her left eyelid. 'No you 'aven't,' she said stoutly. 'You 'avent got any proper bedding in the spare room now, 'ave you?'

'That's too thin,' I said decidedly. Yet even as I spoke I clutched at the straw and, holding on to it, went at once and wrote to Marion.

'You must come home at once,' I commanded, 'in spite of great-aunt Jane's rheumatism. Is it not written that it is better to have one rheumatic great-aunt than a brother, sister-in-law, and a niece in an asylum!'

For answer Marion wired the time of her return train, and I began to grow hopeful.

'An' when Miss Marryun comes,' remarked Elizabeth, 'if I wos you I wouldn't say nothin' to 'er about the way Mr. Roarings went after Miss 'Arringay.'

'Why not?' I asked involuntarily.

'She mightn't trust 'im arter that. I never thort myself 'e'd turn as quick as 'e did. But men is queer, as my pore mother often said when father give 'er a black eye just to show 'ow fond 'e was of her like. No, the best thing to do is to let Miss Marryun think that Mr. Roarings is still taken up with 'er and only went after the other young lady to make 'er jealous.'

There was much wisdom in Elizabeth's words. Nevertheless, I did not intend to mix myself up in any more matrimonial schemes. Much as I desired to see Marion happy, I felt that arranging the destiny of others did not leave me enough leisure to arrange my own, besides interfering with my literary work. At the moment, too, the thought uppermost in my mind was how to dispose of Gladys.

I went to her with Marion's telegram in my hand and a falsely contrite expression on my face. 'I'm so awfully sorry, Gladys, but a most unforeseen thing has happened,' I said. 'Marion is coming to-day, and she'll have to take your room. Isn't it an idiotic situation?'

Gladys pondered. 'But you have another spare room, haven't you?' she demanded brightly.

'Yes, Gladys, we have. But we haven't got the bedding for that just now. The mattress is being cleaned, and I suppose it won't be sent back for another fortnight at least.'

Undaunted, Gladys had another idea. 'Then do you think Marion would mind sharing my room?'

'She would indeed - you see she walks in her sleep,' I said glibly, wondering how it was George Washington had found any difficulty in dissembling, 'and she's very sensitive about any one getting to know about it.'

Gladys went after that. Henry and I have both decided that we're not going to interfere with incompatibles in future. It's too much of a strain on the nervous system.

Florence A. Kilpatrick

CHAPTER XVIII

Being a further extract from the diary of Miss Marion Warrington. It seemed particularly unfortunate that I should be called away so hurriedly to the bedside of dear Aunt Jane at the very moment of the blossoming of my first real love episode. Yes, I must admit my feelings have undergone a change regarding Mr. Rawlings, whom I call my silent lover.

Evidently he has, all the time, been fated for me. Truly, as the poet says, there's a Divinity that shapes our ends, rough-hew them how we will. Divinity, so to speak, has shaped Mr. Rawlings' rough ends and completely transformed him. After seeing him without his beard and, above all, realizing what sacrifices he has made for my sake, I cannot but be touched by such overwhelming devotion.

There is something almost sublime in the way that man has thrown off the habits of a lifetime for my sake! To think he has even donned white spats to please me! Netta has been trying for ten years to get Henry to wear them, but he remains as obdurate about it as ever.

I was relieved when (the malady of Aunt Jane having somewhat abated) I was able to go back to town after an urgent message from Netta asking me to return at once. No doubt Mr. Rawlings inspired that message. He is a timid lover, but unusually full of resource. Though, for example, he seems afraid to approach me, he actually engaged in a mild flirtation with Gladys Harringay to awaken my interest in him. His intention was so obvious that I found it actually amusing. Any one could see through it. Poor fellow, perhaps he thinks the idea of evoking love by first arousing jealousy is a new one. He is an infant in such matters. I intend him to remain so.

Thursday: I have neglected my diary for nearly a fortnight, for I have been too troubled about Mr. Rawlings to concentrate on anything else. He is certainly a most remarkable man. Though obviously suffering he shrinks from any declaration. Often we are alone for hours (I have asked dear Netta to give him the necessary opportunity to unburden himself) and he does nothing but stare at me in a fixed and dreadful way, and remains mute. Of course I know that I am to blame on account of my former indifference - even antagonism - to him. He is afraid of rebuff. I have extended encouragement to him by all the slight means in my power, and Netta has openly handed him my photo, observing that she knew he would like to have it. I have even gone to the length of asking Henry to convey to him that he has nothing to fear; but Henry resolutely refuses to touch on the subject with him. I cannot understand why, when the happiness of two people is at stake.

Sunday: I don't know what impelled me to do it. Perhaps it was the remembrance of an article of Netta's I once read entitled, 'Should Women Propose?' where she cited the historic instance of Queen Victoria, in whose case, on account of her rank, it was a necessity. I had begun to realize that William was not likely to bring his courage to the sticking point without a great deal of encouragement. Distasteful as the idea was to me, I did not intend to shrink from what I felt was to be my duty. If he, though languishing for love, was too faint-hearted to propose, I saw that it would be necessary for me to undertake that task.

Last evening, therefore, when he called I received him in the drawing-room and explained that Netta and Henry had gone out to the theatre. He at once made for the door, saying in that case he would not stop, but I intercepted him. Closing the door, I said gently, 'I am going to ask you to keep me

Florence A. Kilpatrick

company for an hour - if,' I added archly, 'it won't bore you.'

In a confused sort of way he assured me it would not, and he sat down and dropped into the silence that is becoming habitual when we are left alone together.

I knitted and he pulled hard at his cigarette. At last I said: 'Why don't you smoke a pipe, Mr. Rawlings? I know you prefer it.'

'No, no,' he said vehemently, 'I would much rather have a cigarette. It's a cleaner habit than pipe-smoking, isn't it?'

I smiled faintly and mentally decided that when we were married I would not allow him to deprive himself of one of his greatest joys for my sake.

There was another long silence and then, feeling extremely nervous, I murmured haltingly, 'I - I - wonder if you missed me when I was away nursing my great sick aunt - I - I - mean my sick great-aunt. Did - did - the time seem long?'

'I - I'm not quite sure,' he stammered, obviously as ill at ease as myself. 'You see, to be perfectly frank, Miss Warrington, I was at the time in love as far as I believe, and it seems a confused period.'

I waited for him to continue, my eyes discreetly lowered. As, however, he did not go on, I raised them again.

'Yes?' I said encouragingly.

'That's all,' he replied. He looked so embarrassed and unhappy, and wore such an imploring expression I realized that now or never I must come to his relief.

I laid down my knitting and leaned forward. 'Mr. Rawlings,' I said impressively - 'or, shall I say William - I have known of the state of your feelings towards me for some time now.'

He raised his head, and there was no disguising the look of hope in his eye. 'Do you really mean that?' he asked eagerly.

I nodded. 'I want to tell you not to be afraid. However harsh I once seemed to you, the sight of your devotion and self-sacrifice has touched me.'

'Devotion - self-sacrifice,' he murmured in a wondering tone.

'As such do I regard them, William. But they have reaped their reward. I . . . how shall I tell you . . . it is so difficult . . .'

I paused in some distress, wondering if Queen Victoria had felt as uncomfortable about it as I did.

'I want to tell you that . . . I love you, William,' I said at last, very softly.

There was an intense silence, broken only by his laboured breathing. The intensity of his emotions was evidently too much for him.

'And so,' I concluded, raising my eyes to his for a moment, 'I am going to be your wife.'

There! It was out at last. Having spoken I lowered my eyes again and did not look at him until I heard him say in a strained kind of voice, 'But - but - this is too much honour. Believe me, Miss Warrington, I am not worthy -'

'I think you are,' I replied softly, 'and isn't that enough?'

'It isn't enough - I assure you it isn't,' he replied. I noted that his eyes had a rather staring look and slight beads of perspiration had broken out on his forehead - he must be a man of strong emotions. 'It would be a most unfair thing for a man like me, with all my shortcomings, to inflict myself on any woman.'

'Don't be too modest about yourself,' I put in encouragingly, and somewhat timidly laying my hand on his, I added, 'I like you as you are.'

'Nothing would induce me to let you sacrifice yourself,' he exclaimed hotly, 'it would be monstrous, intolerable!' He sprang to his feet as he spoke. 'I must go at once,' he went on, 'we can never meet again, never, never!'

I rose also, going rather pale. In that moment a dreadful thought came to me that perhaps I had made a mistake. Yet there could have been no misconstruing what he had said to Elizabeth regarding his passion for me.

'Stop, William!' I cried as he retreated to the door, 'why are you so obtuse? Don't you understand how difficult you are making everything for me - as well as for yourself! What is all this talk of sacrifice and your unworthiness. I don't think you are unworthy. I - I - love you - isn't it enough when I say that?'

Involuntarily I stretched out my hands to him as I spoke. He has told me since that the sight of me standing there bathed in the light of the rose-shaded lamp, my eyes and lips unusually soft and tender (so he says), with my arms held out to him, forms a picture that he will never forget. He looked at me for a moment in absolute silence, and appeared to be thinking deeply. When at last he spoke he made an astonishing remark. 'What does it matter about me, after all?' he murmured slowly, as if speaking to himself. 'Good God, little woman, I was just about to act the part of a consummate cad and coward!'

He then strode up to me and continued in a serious tone: 'If you care enough for me to take me with all my faults, I shall be proud to be your husband.'

After which he bent and kissed me very gravely on the forehead, and surprised me by walking out of the room. It was the most remarkable proposal. But then, in every way, my dear William is a most remarkable man.

CHAPTER XIX

There was something distinctly puzzling about Marion's engagement to William. It was William who puzzled me. Instinctively I knew he was not happy. Had I been instrumental in bringing about the match, I should have felt disturbed, but as it happened, they pulled it off without the slightest assistance from me. It is the best way. I am steadily determined never to involve myself in matrimonial schemes for any one in future. Even when The Kid gets old enough to have love affairs, she will get my advice and sympathy, but no active co-operation on my part.

But to return to William. Though he seemed plunged in gloom, Marion was radiant. She gaily prepared her trousseau, and took William on long shopping expeditions from which he returned more overcast than ever. Sometimes I wondered if he had really got over his infatuation for Gladys, and if he had merely proposed to Marion out of pique. A strange foreboding came over me that all was not going well.

This was deepened when Marion came to me one day with her eyes red as though she had been weeping.

'Is anything wrong?' I inquired, an instinctive fear gripping at my heart. 'You surely haven't quarrelled with William?'

She shook her head. 'Can you imagine William quarrelling with any one?'

Florence A. Kilpatrick

I could not. He is one of those comfortable people with whom you can be perfectly frank and outspoken without fear of giving the slightest offence. If I say to him when he is deep in a learned discussion with Henry, 'Do shut up, William, I can't think when you're talking,' he does not snort, glare at me, breathe hard or show any other signs of inward resentment. He at once relapses into silence - an affable silence, not the strained kind when the offended party takes deep respirations through the nose - and I am allowed to think without interruption. It is one of the reasons why I have never minded Henry having him about the place at any time.

'Then if you and William haven't quarrelled, what is wrong?' I asked of the drooping Marion.

'It's - it's about our wedding, Netta. He wants to know if I'll put it off for another six months.'

I started. 'Why should he wish to do that now, with all arrangements made?'

'I don't know. There isn't the slightest reason for delay. It isn't a case of money, for you know he has a good private income, and I have my own little income as well. Then, we are both old enough to know our own minds - yet he says he thinks we ought to have more time for reflection. What can it mean, Netta?'

I was silent for a moment, not liking to voice my uneasy thoughts.

'It isn't that I mind the extra six months' delay,' she went on, 'but I don't like the idea of postponing the wedding. There is something unlucky about it.'

'You're right - it is unlucky,' said the voice of Elizabeth, coming unexpectedly into the discussion.

'Elizabeth,' I said sternly, 'do you mean to tell me you

were listening?'

She drew herself up with dignity. 'Me listenin'! I've too much to do to go poking myself into other people's bizness. But I wos just comin' in to ask wot you wanted for dinner -'

'I have already given orders for dinner, Elizabeth.'

'Well, I musta forgotten 'em. An' just as I was comin' in I 'eard Miss Marryun talkin' about Mr. Roarings wantin' to put the weddin' orf. Don't you let 'im do it, miss. I've 'eard o' young women puttin' off their weddin's so long that in the end they've never took place at all. I've 'ad it 'appen to myself, so I *know*.'

'Elizabeth,' I interposed, 'we don't want your advice. Go away at once.'

'I ain't done yet. You'll be glad o' my advice in the end. Experience 'elps a lot. Some men wot's goin' to be married gets a sort o' funk at the last minnit and, bless you, they'd wriggle out o' it, yes, even if they was goin' to marry an angel out o' 'eaven. My friend's 'usband was one o' them sort - wanted to stop the 'ole thing with the weddin' cake ordered, an' lodgings taken at Margate for the 'oneymoon. But she 'eld 'im to it - stuck to 'im like grim death until' e'd gone through with it. An' now 'e often ses 'e never regrets it for a minnit.'

Marion looked up hopefully. 'Perhaps you're right, Elizabeth.'

'O' course I'm right,' she asserted, throwing a triumphant glance at me as she retired.

'These tactics may be all very well for the lower classes,' I said to Marion when we were alone, 'but I'm not quite sure whether they'd answer in every case. No, Marion dear, if William wants to postpone the wedding, it must be done.'

Her face fell at once, and she looked so dejected I felt troubled.

'If you like I will talk to William and try to discover the reason for his change of plan,' I conceded reluctantly, 'but you must understand, dear, that nothing will make me interfere with the natural course of events.'

Rather to my surprise, William touched on the subject the next time he came to see me. We were sitting alone and I was mentally noting his air of depression, when he suddenly burst out: 'Tell me, frankly, do you think a man is justified in - er - postponing a great event in his life - such as, say, his wedding, if he feels uncertain?'

'Uncertain about what?' I asked gently.

'About himself - and everything, you know. True, Johnson has said that marriage is one of the means of happiness - a sentiment delivered, no doubt, by the great master when he was in a light vein - but supposing a man is not sure that he can make a woman happy -'

'And supposing instead of the hypothetical man and woman you are speaking of, we simply quote the case of you and Marion,' I interposed. 'Am I to understand that you do not wish to marry her?'

He started. 'It isn't exactly that. But at the - er - time I - er - offered myself to Marion I had not weighed all the possibilities. To be perfectly frank with you, I am not quite certain of my own affections. I decided that, with companion-ship, these might develop after marriage. But supposing they do not, then I shall have rendered her unhappy. Is not the risk too great?'

He leaned forward and laid his hand on mine with an expression of great earnestness. 'In this matter,' he said slowly, 'I intend to abide by your decision. I have supreme faith in your judgment, and I do not believe you would advise me wrongly. Tell me what I ought to do. Do you think it is making for the happiness of two people if they are united under these peculiar circumstances?'

'I said I would never interfere,' I began weakly.

'It isn't a question of interfering,' he broke in, 'but only a matter of advising what you think is right or wrong.'

I hesitated, feeling the responsibility keenly. It is true that I am accustomed to giving advice on these delicate matters. In my capacity of writer on the Woman's Page I often discuss affairs of the heart, getting much correspondence on the subject and (if a stamped addressed envelope is enclosed) giving unsparing help and assistance to perplexed lovers. But this case seemed entirely different. It lacked any element of the frivolous. I knew that Manor's whole happiness depended on my answer.

Supposing I suggested that the marriage should go on and afterwards the couple turned out to be totally unsuited, what a serious situation I should have created. As a matter of fact, I more than once suspected that they were incompatibles, but hoped that they would ultimately accommodate themselves to each other. If, however, they did not, I should be confronted with the spectacle of two most excellent people (apart) being thoroughly unhappy (together) for the remainder of their lives. I shivered before the prospect, and was on the point of telling William that I would never advise a union to take place unless there was perfect understanding and sympathy between a couple, when he spoke again.

'It's just at the last minute all these doubts have assailed me,' he explained. 'I didn't realize before how serious a thing marriage is - how irrevocable.'

In a flash Elizabeth's words came into my mind. I recalled her references to men who get in a 'funk' and want to stop proceedings on the eve of the wedding, and then I saw the whole thing. William was that sort of man. I had an instinctive idea just then that no matter who he was going to marry he would have come to me at the eleventh hour with the same

Florence A. Kilpatrick

bewildered demand for advice.

In that moment I decided to trust to Elizabeth. She seems to have a rude knowledge of life which is almost uncanny at times, but entirely convincing. She has, as it were, a way of going to the heart of things and straightway extracting truth. I felt just then that I could depend on her judgment.

'William,' I said, looking at him steadily in the eye, 'you want my candid opinion?'

'I do,' he replied fervently.

'Then I advise you to go on with the marriage. I have weighed it all up, and I feel it is for the best.'

He wrung my hand silently, and then he rose. 'Thank you,' he said, 'I am sure you are always right.' I thought I detected a note of relief in his voice. Man is a perplexing creature.

The next day Marion came to me overjoyed. 'It's all right, dear,' she announced. 'William wants to get married at once. Netta, you are wonderful - how did you do it? What did you say to him?'

'Never mind,' I said, trying to look enigmatical and rather enjoying Marion's respectful admiration of my wondrous powers, 'all's well that ends well . . . ask Elizabeth if it isn't,' I added as that worthy lurched in with the tea-tray.

'The wedding isn't going to be postponed after all, Elizabeth,' announced Marion gleefully.

'I knowed it wouldn't be, Miss Marryun, when I see a weddin' wreath in your cup. I tell you the Signs is always right.'

Marion shook her head. 'Not always. Didn't you once tell me that my future husband would cross water to meet me? Mr. Rawlings, now, has been here all the time.'

Elizabeth paused in the act of arranging the tea-table, and stood in a prophetic attitude with the teapot held aloft.

'Oo ses the Signs is wrong?' she demanded. 'Isn't Mr. Roarings an Irishman, an' was born in Dubling? Now I'd like to know 'ow any one can get from Ireland to London without crossin' water, anyway!'

Marion bowed her head, meekly acquiescent. 'I never thought of that, Elizabeth. You always seem to be right.'

CHAPTER XX

I had not seen Marion and William since their marriage as they had gone on a six-months' tour of the Italian lakes, but I was haunted with the foreboding that the match was not, after all, turning out a success.

For one thing, Marion's silence regarding her marriage was unusual. She wrote only brief notes that made no reference to William. As for William, he did not write at all.

Now Marion is what you would call an ardent correspondent, as well as being a communicative person. If she were happy she would be likely to write no less than eight pages three times a week breathing praise of William - I mean that would be the general tone of her letters. But now she devoted herself exclusively to descriptions of scenery and relating episodes regarding the constant losing and regaining of their baggage on their journeys, which though in its way instructive, struck me as lacking vital interest.

The affair troubled me, because I knew that I was, in a measure, responsible for the match. William had left the decision in my hands, and, on thinking it over, it struck me as a rather cowardly thing to do. What right had he to put it on to me? I knew that if they were not happy I should be haunted by remorse to the end of my days. It was an annoying situation.

When they arrived home and wired from an hotel in London

that they were coming up to see me the next day my trepidation increased. Supposing they came to me with reproaches, even recriminations? I awaited their visit in a subdued frame of mind.

Not so Elizabeth. Her jubilant air, her triumphant expression when she spoke of the newly wedded pair, ended by irritating me.

'Getting married isn't the only thing in life; as you seem to think,' I said rather severely, after a remark of hers that she was glad to think Marion was so happily settled.

'Maybe not, but it's the best,' she commented, 'an' as I always sed about Miss Marryun -'

'Mrs. Rawlings,' I corrected.

'Lor', I'll never get used to the name. Mrs. Roarings, then, 'as only got me to thank for the present 'appy state o' things.'

'What do you mean?' I asked, only half interested.

'Well, it's like this yeer,' answered Elizabeth, 'I see from the very first that Mr. Roarings an' Miss Marryun were just suited to each other. The trouble was they didn't see it theirselves, an' so I 'elped to open their eyes like.'

'Explain,' I commanded.

Elizabeth did so. She unfolded a tale that, as she proceeded step by step, left me speechless with horror. That she should have so basely conspired to throw William and Marion at each other and, by misrepresentations, lies and every kind of deception, brought about the match, utterly appalled me. Everything suddenly became clear. William had married through a misplaced sense of chivalry - offered himself up as a sacrifice as it were. I understood then why Marion had written so much about luggage and nothing about connubial bliss - the union was bound to turn out a ghastly failure under such circumstances. Worst of all, I, quite unconsciously, had aided and abetted the whole disgraceful scheme.

'Elizabeth!' I exclaimed at last in dismay, 'you shameless, intriguing creature, I will never forgive you for this. You have ruined two lives, and I am involved in it as well. The only thing to do is to explain the whole situation to Mr. and Mrs. Rawlings when they come to-day.'

She changed colour. 'You'd never do that, 'm.'

'I shall tell them everything. It will, at any rate, help them to begin life on a different understanding.'

'But what good will that do, 'm? It'll upset everything an' lead to goodness knows wot.'

'It may lead to a judicial separation, of course,' I replied, 'but my duty in this case is perfectly clear. There is only one thing to be done.'

I have never seen the girl so genuinely distressed. 'I wouldn't do it, if I wos you, I wouldn't indeed. If you must tell 'em, wait a year or two, till they've settled down -'

A loud knock on the door interrupted her. 'There they are now,' I remarked. 'And no matter what you say I shall explain everything before they leave to-day. They shall know how they've been hoodwinked.'

'Orl right, then,' said Elizabeth, 'an' let the consingquences be on your own head. You'll see 'ow they'll take it.' And darting defiant looks, she went to open the door.

The next moment Marion was enfolded in my arms. Then I turned to greet William. As I did so the words of welcome died on my lips and I stood staring at him in puzzled wonder.

'Why, what has happened to you?' I asked.

He grinned. 'Don't you like me as I am at present?'

I did not, but thought it polite to refrain from saying so. He had gone back to his former state of fuzziness, and looked more like Rip van Winkle than ever. Indeed, his beard seemed even more fierce and bristly than in the old days - probably shaving had tended to strengthen the roots.

'How do you do, William?' I said, extending my hand, deciding as I did so that I would not give him any other kind of salute after all. Yet it was with a tinge of regret I thought of that nice mouth of his hidden under such a rank undergrowth of whisker.

Marion looked on complacently as I greeted him. I remembered then that she had rather seemed to resent the sisterly salute I thought necessary to bestow on him after the wedding, and the brotherly salutes (repeated four times in succession) he had given me in return. I decided at that moment I would respect her objections and only shake hands with William in future. I am sure she preferred it, and I should hate to displease her.

Besides, beards do rasp one so.

Henry now emerged from the study full of hearty greeting and *bonhomie*. He seemed less surprised at William's altered appearance than I did, and was certainly more pleased about it.

'What made you let him do it?' I said reproachfully to Marion when we were alone, 'he was a really handsome man before, and now -'

'That's just it,' she interrupted, 'he was too handsome, and it wasn't safe for him.'

'Not safe, Marion?'

'Women wouldn't leave him alone - they all flirted with him. It would have been all right if he'd been used to it before, but getting good-looking so suddenly unbalanced him. From a kind of puzzled wonder that he should thus attract the opposite sex, he began to develop an interest in what he termed "their bewildering number of types." He said he used to think they were all exactly alike. It was when he declared his intention of writing a eulogy on woman that I stepped in and insisted on his letting his beard grow again. Don't you think I acted for the best?'

'No doubt you did,' I said pensively, 'but he had such an attractive mouth.'

Marion regarded me severely. 'That's what all the other women seemed to think. I feel I was justified in protecting him.'

'No doubt you were, dear,' I murmured, with meekly lowered eyes. 'Don't you ever regret him as he was before?'

She sighed a little. 'Sometimes - particularly when dear William was just beginning to grow again - did I have my qualms of discouragement. A beard in its incipient stages is an unbecoming, almost startling affair, Netta. Then of course, I find solace by looking at this,' and she held out a small locket containing a portrait of William in his glorified state. 'Also I always keep his white spats and lavender gloves as a remembrance.'

There was a hint of sadness in the idea. It seemed almost as if William was dead - one phase of him was, at all events.

'Then you *do* regret -' I began.

'I regret nothing, Netta,' she broke in very decidedly. 'I am now getting quite reconciled to dear William's present appearance, and I know he's happier in his natural state.'

This was obviously true. William, his feet once more installed on the mantelpiece, pulling hard at his pipe (filled for him by Marion's loving hands) was a picture of perfect contentment.

But it was some time before I ventured to put the question to him that was uppermost in my thoughts.

'Are you happy, William?' I asked tensely when, for a moment, we were alone. 'Was my advice for better or for worse?'

He took my hand and wrung it warmly. 'My dear Netta!' he exclaimed, 'what a fool I was to hesitate even for a moment. Had it not been for you - and, I think I ought to add, Elizabeth - I might never have won such a treasure as my dear Marion. "Marriage," as Dr. Johnson has said, "is the best state for man in general," and although he added that it is more necessary to a man than a woman as he is less able to supply himself with domestic comforts, I think in that case it is put too crudely. I look upon it as something higher and nobler.'

'That's all right, then,' I said, relieved. 'Dr. Johnson seems to have as sound a philosophy as Elizabeth.'

As I sat meditating before the fire that evening, after the departure of the happy couple, Elizabeth entered. Her face betokened anxiety. 'You - you - didn't tell 'em anything, I 'ope?' she demanded.

'Under the circumstances I did not, Elizabeth. They seemed quite happy and so -'

'"Let sleepin' dogs lie,"' she supplemented.

'You seem able to lie a great deal more than sleeping dogs,' I said severely. 'In future, remember to stick to the truth or you may get yourself - and other people - into serious trouble.'

'Right-o, 'm. But Mr. Roarings seemed satisfied enough. Look wot 'e gave me to-day?' - she held out two crisp banknotes. ''E sed they were for my own troosoo,' she added gleefully.

'What, Elizabeth, are you going to be married next?' asked Henry, as he strolled into the room at that moment.

'Well, I ain't got a party in view as yet, sir. But as I always ses, you never know wot a day may bring forth. The Signs 'ave been good for me lately. Isn't there a sayin' somewhere about not knowing the day nor the 'our when the young man may come along? Well, I always think it's best to be prepared, like.'

She went out, but returned a moment later bearing a tray in her hand.

'What is this?' I inquired.

'I thort p'raps you'd like to drink to the occashun of the 'appy 'ome-coming in a nice glarss o' stout,' she explained.

I noted that there were three glasses. 'Elizabeth,' I said coldly, 'you are unduly familiar. I protest -'

'Oh, hang it all, let's be democratic,' put in Henry, grinning. 'It's only your *joie de vivre* and natural *bonhomie*, isn't it, Elizabeth?'

'Not 'arf,' replied Elizabeth. 'Well,' she added a moment later as she raised her glass, "ere's to us, all of us, an' may we never want nothin', none of us - nor me neither.'

I saw that Henry was grappling with the construction of the sentence, and it was a full minute and a half before he gave it up. Then he lifted his glass. 'Thank you, Elizabeth,' he said, 'and the same to you.'

Choose from Thousands of 1stWorldLibrary Classics By

A. M. Barnard
Ada Leverson
Adolphus William Ward
Aesop
Agatha Christie
Alexander Aaronsohn
Alexander Kielland
Alexandre Dumas
Alfred Gatty
Alfred Ollivant
Alice Duer Miller
Alice Turner Curtis
Alice Dunbar
Allen Chapman
Ambrose Bierce
Amelia E. Barr
Amory H. Bradford
Andrew Lang
Andrew McFarland Davis
Andy Adams
Anna Alice Chapin
Anna Sewell
Annie Besant
Annie Hamilton Donnell
Annie Payson Call
Annie Roe Carr
Annonaymous
Anton Chekhov
Arnold Bennett
Arthur Conan Doyle
Arthur M. Winfield
Arthur Ransome
Arthur Schnitzler
Atticus
B.H. Baden-Powell
B. M. Bower
B. C. Chatterjee
Baroness Emmuska Orczy
Baroness Orczy
Basil King
Bayard Taylor
Ben Macomber
Bertha Muzzy Bower
Bjornstjerne Bjornson
Booth Tarkington
Boyd Cable
Bram Stoker
C. Collodi
C. E. Orr

C. M. Ingleby
Carolyn Wells
Catherine Parr Traill
Charles A. Eastman
Charles Amory Beach
Charles Dickens
Charles Dudley Warner
Charles Farrar Browne
Charles Ives
Charles Kingsley
Charles Klein
Charles Hanson Towne
Charles Lathrop Pack
Charles Romyn Dake
Charles Whibley
Charles Willing Beale
Charlotte M. Braeme
Charlotte M. Yonge
Charlotte Perkins Stetson
Clair W. Hayes
Clarence Day Jr.
Clarence E. Mulford
Clemence Housman
Confucius
Coningsby Dawson
Cornelis DeWitt Wilcox
Cyril Burleigh
D. H. Lawrence
Daniel Defoe
David Garnett
Dinah Craik
Don Carlos Janes
Donald Keyhoe
Dorothy Kilner
Dougan Clark
Douglas Fairbanks
E. Nesbit
E.P.Roe
E. Phillips Oppenheim
Earl Barnes
Edgar Rice Burroughs
Edith Van Dyne
Edith Wharton
Edward Everett Hale
Edward J. O'Biren
Edward S. Ellis
Edwin L. Arnold
Eleanor Atkins
Eliot Gregory

Elizabeth Gaskell
Elizabeth McCracken
Elizabeth Von Arnim
Ellem Key
Emerson Hough
Emilie F. Carlen
Emily Dickinson
Enid Bagnold
Enilor Macartney Lane
Erasmus W. Jones
Ernie Howard Pie
Ethel May Dell
Ethel Turner
Ethel Watts Mumford
Eugenie Foa
Eugene Wood
Eustace Hale Ball
Evelyn Everett-green
Everard Cotes
F. H. Cheley
F. J. Cross
F. Marion Crawford
Federick Austin Ogg
Ferdinand Ossendowski
Francis Bacon
Francis Darwin
Frances Hodgson Burnett
Frances Parkinson Keyes
Frank Gee Patchin
Frank Harris
Frank Jewett Mather
Frank L. Packard
Frank V. Webster
Frederic Stewart Isham
Frederick Trevor Hill
Frederick Winslow Taylor
Friedrich Kerst
Friedrich Nietzsche
Fyodor Dostoyevsky
G.A. Henty
G.K. Chesterton
Gabrielle E. Jackson
Garrett P. Serviss
Gaston Leroux
George A. Warren
George Ade
Geroge Bernard Shaw
George Durston
George Ebers

George Eliot	Herbert Carter	John Habberton
George Gissing	Herbert N. Casson	John Joy Bell
George MacDonald	Herman Hesse	John Kendrick Bangs
George Meredith	Hildegard G. Frey	John Milton
George Orwell	Homer	John Philip Sousa
George Sylvester Viereck	Honore De Balzac	Jonas Lauritz Idemil Lie
George Tucker	Horace B. Day	Jonathan Swift
George W. Cable	Horace Walpole	Joseph A. Altsheler
George Wharton James	Horatio Alger Jr.	Joseph Carey
Gertrude Atherton	Howard Pyle	Joseph Conrad
Gordon Casserly	Howard R. Garis	Joseph E. Badger Jr
Grace E. King	Hugh Lofting	Joseph Hergesheimer
Grace Gallatin	Hugh Walpole	Joseph Jacobs
Grace Greenwood	Humphry Ward	Jules Vernes
Grant Allen	Ian Maclaren	Julian Hawthrone
Guillermo A. Sherwell	Inez Haynes Gillmore	Julie A Lippmann
Gulielma Zollinger	Irving Bacheller	Justin Huntly McCarthy
Gustav Flaubert	Isabel Hornibrook	Kakuzo Okakura
H. A. Cody	Israel Abrahams	Kenneth Grahame
H. B. Irving	Ivan Turgenev	Kenneth McGaffey
H.C. Bailey	J.G.Austin	Kate Langley Bosher
H. G. Wells	J. Henri Fabre	Kate Langley Bosher
H. H. Munro	J. M. Barrie	Katherine Cecil Thurston
H. Irving Hancock	J. Macdonald Oxley	Katherine Stokes
H. Rider Haggard	J. S. Fletcher	L. A. Abbot
H. W. C. Davis	J. S. Knowles	L. T. Meade
Haldeman Julius	J. Storer Clouston	L. Frank Baum
Hall Caine	Jack London	Latta Griswold
Hamilton Wright Mabie	Jacob Abbott	Laura Dent Crane
Hans Christian Andersen	James Allen	Laura Lee Hope
Harold Avery	James Andrews	Laurence Housman
Harold McGrath	James Baldwin	Lawrence Beasley
Harriet Beecher Stowe	James Branch Cabell	Leo Tolstoy
Harry Castlemon	James DeMille	Leonid Andreyev
Harry Coghill	James Joyce	Lewis Carroll
Harry Houidini	James Lane Allen	Lewis Sperry Chafer
Hayden Carruth	James Lane Allen	Lilian Bell
Helent Hunt Jackson	James Oliver Curwood	Lloyd Osbourne
Helen Nicolay	James Oppenheim	Louis Hughes
Hendrik Conscience	James Otis	Louis Tracy
Hendy David Thoreau	James R. Driscoll	Louisa May Alcott
Henri Barbusse	Jane Austen	Lucy Fitch Perkins
Henrik Ibsen	Jane L. Stewart	Lucy Maud Montgomery
Henry Adams	Janet Aldridge	Luther Benson
Henry Ford	Jens Peter Jacobsen	Lydia Miller Middleton
Henry Frost	Jerome K. Jerome	Lyndon Orr
Henry James	John Burroughs	M. Corvus
Henry Jones Ford	John Cournos	M. H. Adams
Henry Seton Merriman	John F. Kennedy	Margaret E. Sangster
Henry W Longfellow	John Gay	Margret Howth
Herbert A. Giles	John Glasworthy	Margaret Vandercook

Margret Penrose
Maria Edgeworth
Maria Thompson Daviess
Mariano Azuela
Marion Polk Angellotti
Mark Overton
Mark Twain
Mary Austin
Mary Catherine Crowley
Mary Cole
Mary Hastings Bradley
Mary Roberts Rinehart
Mary Rowlandson
M. Wollstonecraft Shelley
Maud Lindsay
Max Beerbohm
Myra Kelly
Nathaniel Hawthrone
Nicolo Machiavelli
O. F. Walton
Oscar Wilde
Owen Johnson
P.G. Wodehouse
Paul and Mabel Thorne
Paul G. Tomlinson
Paul Severing
Percy Brebner
Peter B. Kyne
Plato
R. Derby Holmes
R. L. Stevenson
R. S. Ball
Rabindranath Tagore
Rahul Alvares
Ralph Bonehill
Ralph Henry Barbour
Ralph Victor
Ralph Waldo Emmerson
Rene Descartes
Rex Beach

Rex E. Beach
Richard Harding Davis
Richard Jefferies
Richard Le Gallienne
Robert Barr
Robert Frost
Robert Gordon Anderson
Robert L. Drake
Robert Lansing
Robert Lynd
Robert Michael Ballantyne
Robert W. Chambers
Rosa Nouchette Carey
Rudyard Kipling
Samuel B. Allison
Samuel Hopkins Adams
Sarah Bernhardt
Sarah C. Hallowell
Selma Lagerlof
Sherwood Anderson
Sigmund Freud
Standish O'Grady
Stanley Weyman
Stella Benson
Stella M. Francis
Stephen Crane
Stewart Edward White
Stijn Streuvels
Swami Abhedananda
Swami Parmananda
T. S. Ackland
T. S. Arthur
The Princess Der Ling
Thomas A. Janvier
Thomas A Kempis
Thomas Anderton
Thomas Bailey Aldrich
Thomas Bulfinch
Thomas De Quincey
Thomas Dixon

Thomas H. Huxley
Thomas Hardy
Thomas More
Thornton W. Burgess
U. S. Grant
Valentine Williams
Various Authors
Vaughan Kester
Victor Appleton
Victoria Cross
Virginia Woolf
Wadsworth Camp
Walter Camp
Walter Scott
Washington Irving
Wilbur Lawton
Wilkie Collins
Willa Cather
Willard F. Baker
William Dean Howells
William le Queux
W. Makepeace Thackeray
William W. Walter
William Shakespeare
Winston Churchill
Yei Theodora Ozaki
Yogi Ramacharaka
Young E. Allison
Zane Grey

www.ingramcontent.com/pod-product-compliance
Lightning Source LLC
Chambersburg PA
CBHW020504100426
42813CB00030B/3114/J